WILD H

A Personal,
One-Day Quest
to Liberate
the Artist and Lover
Within

A FIRESIDE BOOK

Published by Simon & Schuster
New York London Toronto Sydney Tokyo Singapore

ELLIOT
SOBEL

EART

DANCING

F

FIRESIDE
Rockefeller Center
1230 Avenue of the Americas
New York, New York 10020

FIRESIDE and colophon are registered trademarks
of Simon & Schuster Inc.

Designed by Hyun Joo Kim
Manufactured in the United States of America

1   2   3   4   5   6   7   8   9   10

Library of Congress Cataloging-in-Publication Data

Sobel, Elliot.
Wild heart dancing : a personal, one-day quest to liberate the
artist and lover within / Elliot Sobel.
p.   cm.
"A Fireside book."
Includes bibliographical references.
1. Spiritual life.   2. Creation (Literary, artistic, etc.)   3. Love.
4. Sobel, Elliot.   I. Title.
BL624.S615   1994
248.4—dc20   93-36248
CIP

ISBN: 0-671-86965-5

Grateful acknowledgment is made to the following for permission to use excerpts from copyrighted work:

New Directions Publishing Corporation, for selections from
Henry Miller on Writing, copyright © 1964 by
Henry Miller.

Bantam Books, a division of Bantam Doubleday Dell Publishing
Group, Inc., for selection from *Bluebeard,* by Kurt Vonnegut,
copyright © 1987 by Kurt Vonnegut.

Thames & Hudson Ltd., for selections from *Sacred Dance,* copyright © 1974 by Maria-Gabriele Wosien.

Selection from *The Paintings of Henry Miller,* reprinted with
permission of Capra Press, 1993.

In deepest gratitude to my beloved parents,
Max and Manya Sobel

Acknowledgments

Special appreciation to:

Gabrielle Roth, shaman, dancer, director, and author, who recognized my artist-soul, liberated my dancing body, insisted I was a writer, and made me do stand-up comedy about my sex life in front of hundreds of strangers on a regular basis!

Asha Greer, a true Artist of Being and "Wild Heart Dancer," in whose loving home and creative presence my painting and music flourished and this book was completed. Her instructions to me when we first met in Jerusalem were that I immediately begin the daily practice of singing a song based on a poem by Rumi, until my life changed:

> Come, come, whoever you are,
> This caravan has no despair.
> Come, come, whoever you are,
> This caravan is not of despair.
>
> Wanderer, worshipper, lover of leaving come.
> Wanderer, worshipper, lover of leaving come.
> Even though you have broken your vows,
> Perhaps ten thousand times,
>
> Still come again, come, whoever you are,
> Whoever you are, come.
>
> (Etc. I came.)

Warren Selinger, who helped create, finance, and co-lead our "Courage of Self-Expression" workshops, which provided much of the inspiration and material for this work. I met him at a party in 1978 when he walked up to me, stuck his hand out, and said, "Hi, my name is Warren and I am free to express myself." Together, we began our work of asking people to do all sorts of silly and creative things for a fee.

Rabbi David Cooper, for his generous and perceptive feedback, which helped this book arrive in its present form, and who, along with his wife, Shoshana, kindly hosted me for three rich months in their beautiful home in Jerusalem.

John Soper, Jessica Britt, Bette Dingman, Nancy Lunney and Pat Lewine of Esalen Institute, Big Sur, California, who provided me with the privilege and opportunity to teach and learn at Esalen.

Marty and Alisun Schrank, beloved friends with whom I lived when writing the original draft of this book, and who are famous in Santa Cruz, California, for their dynamite barbecues. On the day of their marriage, I dropped the wedding cake on the sidewalk; they still allow me to visit.

Darsi Kamay, the tantric playmate who got away, who has promised to write a full exposé of my shortcomings for the *National Enquirer* in the event I am ever well known.

The Lama Foundation, Ram Dass, and all my Lama friends for consistently providing a sacred space of love, spiritual nourishment, and retreat.

My brother, Harry, with whom I once co-authored a generally terrible unpublished novel about elephant waste; my sister-in-law, Wendy, who was once described by a relative as being "better than nothing"; my nieces, Julie and Amy, who once told me that I was the most immature grown-up they had ever met, which pleased me greatly.

Other teachers along the way, including Werner Erhard, Stewart Emery, Carol Augustus, and the late Hilda Charlton. Having come to New York to live and write in 1976, I promptly developed a creative block and a depression. I went to one of Hilda's meetings at the Cathedral of St. John the Divine, along with some three or four hundred others, and afterward, having never laid eyes on me, she marched up to me, bopped me on the chest and said, "Whatsa matter kid, depressed? Why don't you write a book!"

Sheila Curry and Laurie Munroe Abkemeier of Simon and Schuster, for skillfully guiding this work, and me, through the publishing process.

In loving memory of Fanny Lerner and Irving Sobel, whose generosity provided me with the leisure time to complete this project; and finally, a heartful thank-you to all the family members and lunatic-fringe friends who together consitute the true meaning of my life, including, in no particular order:

Perry Goldstein, Jana Wolff, Eddie Greenberg, David Gilbert, Monica Maclean, Mary Mooney, Douglas Day, Steve Kennedy, Sharon Lowinger, Michael Freeman, Marty Rubenstein, Cheryl Schwartz, Maria Higgins, Charlie Castelli, Michael Chadwick, Randy Smith, Stephanie Gilbert, Jill Castelli, Reb Charles Horowitz, Charley Wininger, Lois Lessler, Janat Dundas, Leslie French, Shivaya, Christina Frith, Arlene Travis, Rabbi Solomon and Glenda Dubin, Michael Wyman, Robert Ansell, "The Mirrors," Marilyn Hover, Susan Sharpe, Lindy Clarke, Anja Buchner, Gerda, Norbert, and the Kassner/Lerner/Sobel extended families. Ellen Lubell, Bill Prevas, Rick Powers, Willa Rothman, Howie Cohn, Karen Gold, Fish, and my neighbors in Virginia: Caitlin, M.B. and Pete, Suzanna, Peter, Sky, Diane, Rania, the infamous Dr. Steven J. Louis Weiner, and the ever-elusive Joey Heavens.

...and last, a special thank-you to author Peter McWilliams for introducing me to my agent, Phil Pochoda; to Phil, for introducing me to my first editor, Gail Winston; and to Gail, for buying this book and making my mother happy.

Every child is an artist, before the artist is conditioned out of it. The child does not look, it sees. Every child is a seer: sees horses, angels, faces in a cloud, senses the spirits in tree and cave. The child is a maker of stories, draws and paints without hesitation, hums and dances its moods... until it is plugged in and the artist is driven underground.

Frederick Franck,
Art as a Way

WILD HEART DANCING

Contents

We are all born geniuses, and some of us grow up less damaged than others.

Buckminster Fuller

WILD HEART DANCING

Vaslav Nijinsky

WILD HEART DANCING

Introduction

*H*idden within every one of us is a mysterious and creative spark of artistry and genius. Life is the ultimate medium for the expression of these qualities, and it is our spiritual task to develop into Artists of Being. This requires both a courageous spirit as well as a poetic soul.

The expressive arts—painting, singing, dancing, writing, and acting—can serve as teachers in our quest for mastery over the creative process in life itself. For daily we face the work-in-progress that is our lives, and daily we have the opportunity to add new colors and shadings. And just as the talented painter is able to translate inner visions to the canvas through skillful brushwork, the Artist of Being can generate living realities through the appropriate application of intuitive choices and action.

Yet the artist within has been driven underground; the genius has been damaged. Rather than joyfully embracing the daily artistic challenge to create beauty on one's life canvas, most of us have already given up and are doing the best we can to suffer with the picture we already created, albeit unconsciously.

Wild Heart Dancing is designed as a one-day personal retreat that combines solitude, self-inquiry, and the expressive arts as a means of gently restoring you to your original and spontaneous artistry and genius. The free-flowing child-artist has not been irreversibly buried. She or he can be coaxed back out. But it requires a particular atmosphere; this book will guide you in providing yourself with the necessary conditions to accomplish this reemergence. Its intent is to assist you in transforming yourself into a lover: one who celebrates life in the living of it. One who dares to sing when others—living in fear—keep silent; one who chooses to dance when others—of sluggish body and soul—prefer watching TV, or worse, watching life; one who writes sonnets and love letters while others—anxious and worried—are filling out forms.

It is our task as spiritual beings to remove the blocks to our natural intoxication, our native passion for life and spirit: to enjoy the hearty laughter and mischief of the cosmic jokers and magicians; to attain the delightful innocence of those rare adults who remain childlike, able to be filled with awe and wonder by the sheer, ineffable mystery of it all; those who take nothing for granted, who know they know nothing at all, and rest in that fundamental bafflement. The "mature" human lover is an infant, gazing wide-eyed at the incomprehensible.

But when the creative spirit has been squashed or insulted in early childhood, it requires enormous courage and vulnerability to dare expose it again. The freedom to express oneself fully and spontaneously—whether in life or art—requires a sense of safety, and an expectation that one's creative offerings will be wholeheartedly received and appreciated for their essence rather than judged for their form, style or technique.

Imagine a three-year-old child returning home from his first day of preschool, proudly carrying a crayon drawing which is little more than a bunch of random shapes and scribbles. Ordinarily, the normal parent will *not* respond by saying, "Thank you, honey, but I really have to say, you clearly lack any sense of composition or design, your approach to color is a bit off, and I think you'd better consider giving up art."

On the contrary, in most cases the work will be proudly displayed on the refrigerator, and conversations with the relatives will begin to include serious discussions of the child's artistic talents. And rightfully so! For whether or not the parents are skilled art critics, they have recognized in their child's work the spark of originality, the freshness of vision which emerges naturally from a child's as yet undamaged connection to life.

And this is the sort of unconditional appreciation we need to give *ourselves,* if we ever expect that innocent spark of creativity to peek out again. We somehow have to trust that just who we are is inherently valid, and has something worth sharing that will not be subjected to evaluations of good or bad. We need to give ourselves permission to simply be who we are, for it then becomes possible to recover the effortless originality of the essential Self. For as Mozart tells us:

> Why my productions take from my hand that particular form and style that makes them *Mozartish,* and different from the works of other composers, is probably owing to the same cause which renders my nose so large or so aquiline, or in short, makes it Mozart's, and different from those of other people. For I really do not study or aim at any originality.[1]

Similarly, the Artist of Being is that person who can "get out of the way"—give up the struggle to be original and creative—and simply *allow* the mysterious and inherently original flow of his own creative energy to be expressed. In other words, we must make it permissible to simply be ourselves again. To remove the protective layers of self-consciousness and fear that prevent the natural expressions of our inner artist and genius—our common birthright.

Part of our problem with successfully meeting the challenge of creative expression is that the technology and media of our times constantly expose us to the works of the great masters in every artistic field, and we therefore often feel hopelessly inadequate by comparison. But there was a time when this wasn't so, and local talent, however humble, was greatly honored and appreciated by the community simply for being a truly heartfelt offering.

I've been told that qualities of this sort of "tribal respect" for creative expression remains intact in places like Bali and other less technological cultures. And I have personally encountered such a community here in the United States, although not in a geographical sense: rather, it is composed of the readers of books such as this one, the people who attend arts workshops and growth seminars, and so forth. We need not be Cézanne to make art, or Rilke to write poetry. We need only be human, vulnerable, and truthful.

Kurt Vonnegut sums all this up quite well in *Bluebeard:*

> ... simply moderate giftedness has been made worthless by the printing press and radio and television and satellites and all that. A moderately gifted person who would have been a community treasure a thousand years ago has to give up, has to go into some other line of work, since modern communications put him or her into daily competition with nothing but world's champions.
>
> The entire planet can get along nicely now with maybe a dozen champion performers in each area of human giftedness. A moderately gifted person has to keep his or her gifts all bottled up until, in a manner of speaking, he or she gets drunk at a wedding and tap-dances on the coffee table like Fred Astaire or Ginger Rogers. We have a name for him or her. We call him or her an "exhibitionist."[2]

This book is an invitation for you to wake yourself from the sleep of mediocrity, passivity, and resignation into which our culture has lulled you, and to begin to express your innate Divinity and greatness once again.

Greatness, however, is not measured in worldly terms; it doesn't mean superstardom, acclaim or wealth. Rather, it means to be a lover. A minstrel and a poet. To risk being thought of as a bit of an eccentric genius, perhaps. Confusing to others. Not fitting in. Having the courage to be fully alive, and to see the world through the eyes of the heart. To boldly be your Self in a world which seems intent on keeping you quiet and unobtrusive, your light dimmed. To become a one-man or one-woman traveling circus act and magic show, and leave your mark of enchantment wherever you go. To give up trying to *find* your Self and dare to commence *being* your Self: the visionary soul, the lover, artist, and genius.

It truly is possible to restore ourselves to this kind of greatness: to be spontaneous again, to celebrate life, to be a singer of love songs and a dancer moving gracefully through the choreography of a human life span. To live as an Artist of Being, strolling down the path of the minstrel-lover. To emerge on the local human scene as a Wild Heart Dancer.

I have suffered from a very bad habit throughout my life. It *23* began at age fourteen, when I read *How to Develop a Million Dollar Personality*. My problem is this: whenever I enter a bookstore, in spite of my best intentions and taste for literature and philosophy, I find myself unconsciously sidling over to the Self-Help section. Once there, I am mesmerized by the hundreds of titles that seem to speak to all of the broken and wounded parts of my psyche, promising to fix them. I can never decide what to work on first: *Heal Your Family System, Enhance Your Romantic Relationships, End Addictive Behavior, Open Your Creative Flow, Channel Your Higher Mind, Release Your Anger, Overcome Your Depression, Talk to Your Parents, Unleash Your Sexual Energy, Learn to Be*. The task of fixing or improving myself seems so hopelessly overwhelming that I end up despairing of even beginning such a monumental project.

Fortunately, most of my friends know this weakness of mine, and if they are with me, they will eventually notice me gazing dumbstruck and paralyzed at the Self-Help shelves, and will gently take my arm and guide me, like a blind man, over to Fiction, or in severe cases, Humor.

I have tried everything in my quest for personal wholeness and healing. Beyond merely reading all those books on how to change my life, I have also attended seminars, workshops, and crash courses, consciousness-raising sessions, awareness programs, and motivation trainings. I've traveled to distant lands, seeking out gurus and saints, teachers, shamans, and holy people. I have learned meditation techniques, sacred mantras, Sanskrit chants, breathing exercises. I have lived in spiritual communities and visited ashrams; studied the lives of yogis and mystics; explored the paths to God-Realization and Enlightenment. I have experimented with positive thinking, affirmations, and creative visualizations; gone to palm readers, astrologers, and tarot card wizards; consulted psychics, mediums, and therapists; tried drugs, sex, and rock and roll.

24

All of these explorations have been generally fascinating, as well as helpful and inspirational, and they often seemed to satisfy the spiritual hunger of many fellow seekers whom I encountered within them. Yet none of them provided any sort of lasting balm for my own particular wounds.

No, for me it was my love affair with the expressive arts that gradually and gently breathed life back into my soul. Through painting my pain, singing my sorrow, dancing my despair, and making poetry of my pleading, I eventually realized that I had stumbled onto a path that actually worked for me: the path of the artist, the path of the minstrel-lover. My heroes and champions on this path were not the self-help gurus, after all, but the poets: no longer interested in reading *How to Live with Yourself,* I turned instead to the Walt Whitmans and Jack Kerouacs pouring out their naked heart confessions. It was not the human potential mavens who would show me the way, but the dancers: the Nijinskys and Isadora Duncans, leaping and whirling through space in fiery bursts of rapture. The sublime music of Bach and Debussy became my guide, the paintings of Renoir my healers, the passionate outbursts of D. H. Lawrence my inspiration.

In the fictional character of Zorba, from *Zorba the Greek,* by Kazantzakis, I saw the embodiment of who I wanted to be: someone fully and vitally alive, spontaneous and adventurous, fearing nothing, appreciating everything. Sensual and free, Zorba was not reading self-help books, or trying to "find himself." He was living his personal quest in an active and passionate way: rather than despairing over his lack of answers, he would just have another glass of wine and shout the questions a little louder! And if still no answers came, why then, he would get out his *santuri* and sing!

We too must come alive again. We need to "be as children," and see life through the eyes of the heart, the eyes *25* of the magical artist, the eyes of innocence and love. This is a seeing which excludes nothing and which allows us to be passionate and wild in the face of the totality of the human condition as it is. And through this capacity to celebrate "the way things are," we may find ourselves serving as a vehicle through which "the way things are" may actually have a chance to improve and heal. Just because we're around.

It is the purpose of this one-day retreat to assist you in contacting the gentle healing power of your own artistic energy, and launch you out of the self-help realm back into the land of the living. Or better stated, the purpose of the day is to "Zorbize" your soul: to awaken you to the magic and mystery of human life, and your innate capacity to enjoy and celebrate the drama of existence through expressing your Self—your love—with courage, artistry, a sense of adventure and humor. I invite you to risk a lover's leap into free-fall/true confession/soul expression; to enter the land of the Wild Heart Dancing.

. . . the mass of men lead lives of quiet desperation. . . . I went to the woods because I wished to live deliberately, to front only the essential facts of life, and see if I could not learn what it had to teach, and not, when I came to die, discover that I had not lived . . . it is easier to sail many thousand miles through cold and storm and cannibals, in a government ship, with 500 men to assist one, then it is to explore the private sea, the Atlantic and Pacific Ocean of one's being alone. . . .[3]

Henry David Thoreau

WILD HEART DANCING

Setting Up Your One-Day Retreat

*I*t is quite possible to conduct a personal retreat in a wide variety of settings; a room in a New York City apartment where you can arrange to be alone and undisturbed for a day will do just as well as an idyllic cabin in the Colorado Rockies. The point is to create an atmosphere of genuine privacy and solitude, no matter where you find yourself.

I recently spent forty days and forty nights living alone in a ten by ten–foot hut atop a mountain in Virginia. I had no running water, electricity, telephone, bathroom, television, or microwave. I collected rainwater in a barrel, cooked over a tiny propane burner, chopped wood for heat, dug a latrine. I spent my days in silence, contemplation, prayer, song, dance, reading, writing, walking, thinking, thinking, and thinking.

And thinking. I became very familiar with my own mind, which, as you can probably imagine, was a very mixed blessing. Silence and solitude are the optimum conditions in which to become aware of the cacophony of mental noise which we carry with us everyday. And quiet retreat time is likewise one of the best methods for remembering and reconnecting to one's deeper Self, and for clarifying one's life direction and higher purpose.

But as Thoreau suggests, being alone with oneself for an extended period of time is not easy. Most of us prefer to keep ourselves continuously distracted and occupied with the business and pleasures of daily living, so as to avoid confronting the chaos of our own minds as well as the beauty and power of our deepest essence.

And yet the rewards of quality "hermitage" time are enormous, and it is for this reason that I designed this book in the form of a one-day retreat. It is an unusual opportunity for you to step back temporarily and get an aerial view of your own life; to relax the ongoing daily struggle for survival and the perpetual effort to "keep it all together," and merely be with yourself, as you are, however and wherever you are, for better or worse.

Retreating in this manner can be potentially peaceful and healing, yet for the many people who are unaccustomed to slowing down, it can also be a somewhat frightening notion. Who knows what inner demons lurk behind the scenes of our jam-packed schedules? Fear? Boredom? Regret? A sense of meaninglessness? Resignation? We need to be willing to confront all of these if we wish to move past them and touch base with our essential Self. But most of us distract ourselves from this process through the constant "doing" of our lives and we completely neglect to attend to the dimension of "being." Yet it is the latter which ultimately determines the quality of our lives.

29

To the extent that your daily life activities are infused with a richness of "Being-Presence," to that extent will you experience meaning, joy, and aliveness. And likewise, to the extent that you are merely going through the motions of life, reluctantly doing what you must because you experience no choice in the matter, then to that extent will you be one of the walking weary, one of the passionless, powerless people who are simply putting up with things, resigned to their fate.

We have all experienced glimpses of another possibility; times when, if just for a moment, we felt more in touch with a sense of awe and gratitude. Perhaps such momentary "peak experiences" occurred as we witnessed a glittering first snowfall on a December dawn, or heard the poignant melody of a solo cello in a Brahms symphony. Whether it was from participating in the birth of our first child, or the initial excitement of a spring love at age seventeen, we suddenly felt our lives to be rich and full and laced through with meaning and purpose. They were times of great energy, vitality, radiant aliveness, love and laughter. Some of us may even have been blessed to experience the rapture of religious ecstasy and spiritual communion, in which we felt the boundaries of our small ego-self dissolve and we felt ourselves to be one with a greater energy field, characterized by great bliss, compassion, and understanding.

Such close encounters with Sacred Mystery, however brief, are usually sufficient to arouse in a person a great spiritual yearning. The taste of the possibility of Radiant Human Life is unforgettable and irresistible: it renders anything less virtually intolerable. Paradoxically, such wondrous moments of vision nearly always involve the sudden capacity to perceive the extraordinary in the ordinary. The mystery and beauty of life—just as it is—is suddenly grasped, whereas a moment before it appeared banal and mundane. Therefore, while most people in this world are busy trying to change and arrange their lives in a way they believe will yield happiness, the deeper yearning for wholeness can be fulfilled in one's present circumstances without any alterations whatsoever, apart from a radical alteration in perception.

And for this, it is necessary to quiet the mind, soften the heart, step back from one's life and from habitual ways of thinking, and awaken intuition and creativity. For all these reasons, I invite you to adhere to the following guidelines in setting up a one-day hermitage for yourself, a day of retreat, contemplation, and creative expression, devoted to the noblest of purposes: being fully alive.

#1: Set aside a whole day to be completely alone, and follow the course set out in this book from start to finish.

I am well aware that this is an extremely demanding commitment, especially for busy people who have very little free time, children to attend to, chores to do around the house, job-related work, social engagements, and so forth. For some of you, it may be the first time in your lives that you've actually taken one full day off from *everything,* and *everyone,* and devoted the entire day to your own life, to cultivating the creative, loving expression of your Self. I know that for many of you it will take a great deal of effort to make whatever arrangements it requires for you to actually have one full day of life on this Earth all to yourself, undisturbed by even a single external demand. Ideally, put yourself in a quiet environment where *no one will be able to see or even hear you.* The presence of other people within earshot may make you self-conscious about doing some of the exercises. You really need to feel free of all such concerns. Obviously, a secluded cabin in the woods would be the optimal situation for this sort of retreat, but I know that that will not be readily available to many of you. Suffice it to say, the more private you can be for this day, the more spaciousness you will experience in which to let down your social persona and relax in the presence of your essential Self.

31

Therefore, *do not see or even speak to anyone for this one day,* and this includes not making telephone calls, reading mail, or writing letters. Again, I know that these may seem like outrageous requests. Who among us, in this frenetic world of ours, can possibly go a whole day without interacting with any of our fellow human beings? Especially those of us with family responsibilities and active households. It's a lot to ask. I mentioned my extended retreat to you earlier as inspiration: if I was able to do it for forty days, you can certainly manage one!

Think of all the time you have given in your life to employers, to friends, to family, to television and movies, to hobbies, to sleep. Surely it is not too much to ask that you give *yourself* just one full day of your time and attention. For it is truly your Self we are talking about—your true Self, your inner authenticity and conscious artistry of Being, without which all the rest of life is a dismal, empty affair anyway.

So please, do whatever it takes to set aside a day on your calendar, free of all cares, worries, concerns, demands, and responsibilities, a true day off from the business of life. (Remember snow days when you were a kid and you got to stay home from school and play all day?)

"Doing whatever it takes" may mean locking yourself in the basement for the day, shipping the kids off to Grandma's for the weekend, or hiring a baby-sitter. It may mean renting a motel room, or simply telling the people with whom you live that you are planning to spend a day in your bedroom and don't wish to be disturbed under any circumstances. It may mean unplugging your phone or putting on your answering machine.

"One full day" may or may not mean spending the night, depending on your situation. Again, if you secure the ideal cottage in the woods, you ought to go for the full experience of a twenty-four-hour hermitage. If you find yourself in a room in your home, count on the retreat taking approximately twelve hours to complete. Begin your day around 9 A.M. if possible. If you finish sooner, take the rest of the day for quiet reflection and contemplation. If you like, you might want to bring a musical instrument or a journal to use at the end of the day.

#2: **Complete all of the exercises, written and otherwise.**

You will come upon various instructions that you will not particularly want to follow. You may convince yourself you don't really need to follow them, that they are superfluous, or that you already know all about that topic. I ask you to complete all of the exercises in the book, no matter how you feel about them, or how silly or irrelevant they seem to you.

It would be best to approach this book with the innocent "beginner's eyes" of a child. This is much easier said than done. Masters of Zen sit in meditation for years and years to attain this simple skill of having what's called a "beginner's mind." The rest of us are so filled with everything we know and think we know that it is nearly impossible for us to simply be childlike again.

#3: Do not use any alcohol or recreational drugs on this day.

Obviously, you want your mind fresh and clear and "untampered with" for this exploration into your inner world and creative Self-expression. Any substance that alters your state will cloud your experience and make it unclear as to whether *you* are producing your results or the substance is doing it for you. Such confusion is obviously disempowering and constitutes Self-sabotage. Again, as an inspiration, when I did my forty-day hermitage, I not only followed this rule, but I also abstained from coffee and animal products, and except for cheating a few times near the end, I stayed off sugar as well. While it is not required, you may choose to prepare for your experience by eliminating alcohol and other substances a few days in advance, or even trying a simple juice fast as a way of preparing yourself both physically and mentally for a day of truly clear thinking and creative expression.

#4: Prepare a bag lunch and dinner.

Bring whatever food you think you might need or want, although I strongly encourage you to eat simple, nutritious, light foods. (If you are hiding out in your home somewhere, committed to not seeing anyone you live with for the day, then you're not going to want to wander into the kitchen when you get hungry.)

#5: Have the following items with you: a pen and pad,

33

a watch or clock, a small five-and-dime set of watercolors, brushes, and some drawing paper (preferably larger than 8½ by 11 inches), a portable cassette or CD player and a selection of twenty to thirty minutes of your favorite dance music. (If you don't have favorite dance music, get it from a friend who does! Or turn to page 174 where I have recommended several recordings.) Wear loose, comfortable clothing.

#6: Choose a favorite song and memorize the lyrics ahead of time. You may need to purchase the sheet music at your local music store in order to do this, or else listen to your recording a dozen times while you transcribe the words.

#7: Do not bring any other reading matter of any kind.

#8: Do not read or skim through the rest of this book until the day you begin.

34

The temptation will be very great to peek ahead and try to get a sense of what this is all about. Doing so will only dilute your experience. You may also try to convince yourself that you can get what you need from this book by just keeping it on your night table and reading a little of it every night at bedtime. I can promise you that that won't work or produce the best results. Why not? Because a large part of the value of this book is going through the process of having to arrange a full day for yourself! Some of you will be amazed at what you will learn about yourself and your priorities in life just in trying to set up this day, long before you've even picked up the book!

But more importantly, reading this at your bedside will not work because this book does not merely convey *information;* rather, it offers guidelines for a one-day, purely *experiential* retreat. Clearly, reading *about* creativity is a far cry from sitting down with a paintbrush and a blank sheet of paper. In other words, if there is any wisdom to be gleaned from this work, it will not come from my words, but from your own insights resulting from having spent a day in solitude, exploring your own interior world and creative Self-expression.

As you progress through your day of retreat and Self-expression, please allow yourself to experience a full range of feelings, thoughts, and reactions. There is no particular way you are supposed to feel, and there is no particular way you are supposed to think. Furthermore, the results of your experience will be unique to you, in accordance with precisely who you are and exactly what it is you need to feel, express, and contemplate. So it is impossible to "blow it" or fail. Just relax and get involved, in the same way you sometimes lose yourself in a good film. There may be parts when you laugh, and parts when you cry, but it is all part of the experience.

35

Thank you for being willing to engage in this rather unusual experiment. I consider it a great privilege to have your undivided attention in this way, and I promise to do my utmost in order to have our time together be truly useful and meaningful for you.

> It is easy in the world to live after the world's opinion; it is easy in solitude to live after our own; but the great man is he who in the midst of the crowd keeps with perfect sweetness the independence of solitude.[4]

> —Ralph Waldo Emerson

(Please do not turn to the next page until the day you begin your retreat)

I must grasp life at its depth.

Vincent van Gogh

WILD HEART DANCING

Welcome

You are about to put together a One Person Show, an all-day theatrical extravaganza, a solo Cabaret-of-the-Heart, a Coffeehouse-of-the-Soul, featuring You, your own Self as Director, Writer, Choreographer, Set Designer, Star Performer, and Audience. As with any production, there will be times when you are on stage, in the glare of the lights, and times when you are off stage, relaxing, reflecting, working on your character, revising the script.

At present, your theater is empty; you have arrived early to get into costume, get a feel for the stage, and to meditate a few moments in order to center yourself. So please get yourself into a comfortable position, with your back straight, take a few deep breaths, and let them out with an audible sigh, and allow yourself to sink into your surroundings in a relaxed way, and to truly arrive.

Look around the room you are in and just mentally note some of the details of your environment: the color of the walls, the texture of the floor or carpeting, the quality of light, whether natural or electric, the furnishings and decorative objects. Just glance around and allow yourself to feel at home in your own personal retreat space.

For today, there is nowhere else you need to be, nothing else you ought to be doing. And hopefully, there is nobody needing anything from you. Become aware of how the prospect of being alone for a day in this unencumbered way makes you feel. Just take stock of your emotional state as you begin this day of solitude, knowing that wherever you are emotionally—delighted, fearful, whatever—is fine and acceptable. Remember that there is no particular way you're supposed to feel today. Or think. Or be. Just who you are, however you are, is sufficient.

In a moment you will need to put the book down and do the following basic breath-awareness meditation:

Sit comfortably with your eyes closed, and pay attention to your breathing. Mentally observe the flow of your breath as it enters your nostrils, and remain observant of your breath as it departs your nostrils a moment later. As you observe your inhalation, mentally say, "In," and as you observe your exhalation, mentally say, "Out." This is a fairly common form of meditation, and you should do it for five minutes, simply as a way of becoming aware of your own thought processes.

But you probably won't be able to follow more than one or two breaths before your mind has seized control of your attention and gotten you totally engrossed in your thoughts. This is not only natural, it is nearly impossible to do otherwise. The "wandering mind" is the well-known culprit of distraction for even the most seasoned and experienced meditators. So after you've closed your eyes and begun to observe your breath, at some point you'll gradually become aware that you are no longer paying any attention to your breath whatsoever, and instead are totally caught up in some thought or another. Whenever you realize that this has occurred, simply remind yourself that your only instruction, and your only job, is to follow your breath, and so at that point simply guide your attention gently back to the observation of breath. This sequence will undoubtedly occur three dozen times during your five-minute attempt at meditation.

Many people assume that meditation is supposed to feel a certain way, or is supposed to transport the practitioner off into a quiet nether zone of inner peace. This is not necessarily the case. There is no particular way that a meditation session is supposed to be: it may be relaxing, or quite the opposite—agitating and distressing. You may experience a calmness of mind, or more likely, you'll become aware of the ongoing inner chaos with which you are always living.

The purpose is to simply become aware of "what is," not to change it, improve it or calm it down. Furthermore, *whatever* you become aware of is fine, including "I'm not aware of anything at all." Therefore, it is impossible to get the "wrong" result.

Please put the book down now and meditate for five minutes.

Thank you. There will be many times throughout the day for longer periods of meditation. This day would be lacking something crucial if there were no periods of emptiness, no quiet time for reflection. As Artists of Being, we need the white canvas of silence in order to appreciate the exquisite colors of our Self-expression.

Before the show begins, take a look at the program below, in order to get an overview of how your time will be distributed during the course of the day. This schedule is extremely flexible and adaptable to your needs. For example, if your circumstances are such that you must start at noon and go to midnight, that is fine. Or, if you are deeply involved in any activity and need more time, by no means let the clock dictate your creative process.

It may well be that you are naturally drawn to explore one art form more deeply than another, and you may wish to redistribute the time accordingly. On the other hand, it is equally important that you proceed through *all* the exercises with a receptive and curious attitude. The very exercise that you are most hesitant to explore may well be precisely the one which provides you with a deep experience of creative "release," once you are willing to move through your resistance.

40

Program

Perhaps you find it contradictory to be simultaneously retreating from the world, and yet putting on a "performance" of sorts. The two notions seem mutually exclusive. To clarify, imagine you are wandering about in the Himalayas of India. In the distance you hear the faint strains of a tamboura echoing over the hilltops. You follow the enchanting sound, and eventually come upon a lone sadhu (or religious aspirant) sitting high up on a rock, chanting devotional songs to God. Gathered around the rock are many people who, like yourself, have been drawn by the ineffable beauty of the music.

The sadhu, for all intents and purposes, is alone, oblivious to the audience, pouring out his or her heart in music and song with no regard to "performance." And yet, the very purity of such an offering draws audiences from far and wide, anxious to "eavesdrop" on this personal expression of true Self. It is in this spirit that solitude and performance are linked in today's experiment. Your goal is to travel quietly inward toward authentic Self, and to express that essence outwardly in artistic ways, without altering it to please anybody other than the imagined audience of your own witnessing consciousness.

42

And so now, without further ado, the house is starting to fill, the orchestra is tuning up, and the curtain is about to rise . . . this is it, you're on, it's showtime!

How beautiful these movements are that we see in animals, plants, waves and winds. All things in nature have forms of motion corresponding to their innermost being. Primitive man still has such movements and, starting from that point, we must try to create a beautiful movement which sets itself in harmony with the motion of the universe. . . . In my dance the artifices of dancing are thrown aside, the great Rhythms of Life are enabled to play through the physical instrument. The profundities of consciousness are given a channel to the light of our social day. . . . Before I die, I want to teach hundreds of children how to let their souls fill their growing bodies with music and love. I never taught my pupils any steps. I never taught myself technique. I told them to appeal to their spirit, as I did to mine. Art is nothing else.[1]

Isadora Duncan

WILD HEART DANCING

Act I: *Dance the Body Electric*

With the creation of the universe the dance too came into being. . . . The round dance of the stars, the constellation of planets in relation to the fixed stars, the beautiful order and harmony in all its movements, is a mirror of the original dance at the time of creation. The dance is the richest gift of the muses to man. Because of its divine origin it has a place in the mysteries and is beloved by the gods. . . .[2]

—Lucian, Second Century A.D.

*O*ur opening number is a dance . . . through movement and gesture alone, you are to communicate the current spiritual, psychic, and emotional state of your soul to the unconditionally receptive "audience" which surrounds you. Think of it as a "state of the union" ballet. To what extent do you enter this day in a state of rapturous union with the Great Mystery of Life? Or to what extent are you painfully separated from your own Essential Being? Is this a day of rejoicing for you, or a sorrowful lamenting of all that is unclear, all that is unfulfilled within you? Will this opening dance intimate that a comedy is about to begin, or a poignant drama? Or perhaps a little of both? Does your dance celebrate the abundance of love you experience or does it cry out in pain from a position of barren loneliness?

Wherever you find yourself along these spectra of feelings, your dance is to express your naked truth intimately and perfectly. It's as if the very Source of Life itself sits alone in the front row of the orchestra, and this is your opportunity to communicate your Essential Being, to express the problems and/or delights of your present condition.

If you are unaccustomed to dancing, this will be a rather awkward opening for your one-person show. *Then simply be awkward and dance awkwardly.* There's no judge out there. A good way to begin is to stand up and simply begin moving your hands and arms, elbows, wrists, and fingers. Then gradually explore using every part of your body, in isolation: your head, face and jaw, shoulders, chest, hips, pelvis, legs, knees, feet. Consciously loosen and move every body part until you can comfortably slip into a more fluid dance in which you need be conscious of nothing at all apart from the passive observation of your own body spontaneously flowing through space, telling your life story in motion.

Sometimes you'll find your body moving slowly and smoothly; other times, perhaps, quickly, and with choppy gestures. Use different parts of the room you're in, which is your stage, as well as different spatial levels, reaching up to the ceiling, or moving prostrate and snakelike along the floor. Express the variety of emotions as they arise: sometimes your dance will be an expression of anger, sometimes joy; you may find yourself dancing an ancient dance of sorrow, or a Dionysian ritual of celebration.

Just drop all preconceptions, all words, all steps, all technique: let your soul be naked before God and dance your dance fully and totally, as if you were delivering your final message and dance were your only method of communication. Allow yourself to be transported out of your thinking mind, your body surrendered to the pulse of the music, dancing by itself, oblivious to you and your ways. The Self-as-Body, daring to Be. Daring to burst into the living moment of the Great Dance, wriggling to God's rhythm, praying with the whole body.

You are not dancing in order to become a great dancer,

or to create a brilliant piece of choreography. You are dancing because you must, because your body needs to release
itself from the bonds of tension and stiffness and blocked
energy, repressed sexual feelings and lost emotions, con-
fused thoughts, an armored heart, and fear. You dance the
dance of freedom, to explode out of yourself into the fluidity
of Essential Being, moving in space. You dance to recover
the spontaneous, unpredictable motion of original Self unfolding naturally, with childlike abandon, free of restraint,
embarrassment, inhibition.

In that moment of true surrender to the dance, there is
no more "dancer." As it has been said, "you dance until the
dancer disappears and only the dance remains." One *is* one's
body, and speaks as a body in the language of dance. At such
times, what was previously some sort of aerobic exercise or
even choreographed "dance" transforms into a dance of
love, fueled by one's wholeness and integrity. It is an inspired state in which all sense of performance dissolves into
pure spontaneity. Paradoxically, it is this quality which per-
meates the most moving performances.

To reach such a state means you must let go of all self-
consciousness, all thoughts of "Here I am, dancing...
hmmm, which foot should I move next? I wonder what I
look like? I need to buy groceries later." Rather, your
thoughts and judgments quiet down and finally disappear
as your body finds the rhythm, and you let yourself get swept
away into the music, so that the music is dancing you rather
than you dancing to the music. As with the most profound
type of sexual experience, you have literally "gone out of
yourself." You have used the ally of dance to unwind your
soul and restore a piece of genuine Self-expression, via the
physical body, your temple.

To dance truly, in this surrendered manner, is a religious
practice. It is the prayer of the physical form, and its expression can range from a painful pleading for union with one's

inner wholeness, to the ecstatic and mindless celebration of the Living Presence of the Life Force as it spontaneously moves through the body.

> ...the body...is the instrument for the transcendent power; and this power is encountered in the dance directly, instantly and without intermediaries. The body is experienced as having a spiritual, inner dimension as a channel for the descent of the power...it is the aim of the mystics 'inner dance' to come face to face with the Silence, the Void...[3]

—Maria-Gabriele Wosien, *Sacred Dance*

You may want to shock your audience by performing this opening dance in the nude—expose the bare essence of your soul as it is embodied in this vulnerable, human form. (When was the last time you stripped naked and did a rain dance in your living room?) As your dance becomes more aerobic and your breathing deepens, please allow sounds to come forth—not words, but grunts, mumbles, shouts, growls, and chants. If you let it happen, such sounds can spontaneously issue forth from deep within the belly and aid in the process of inner release.

One last note before you begin: I once attended a rigorous dance workshop, and to my great unhappiness, I threw my back out on the very first night. (Not from dancing—from making my bed!) I spent the next day at the workshop sitting on the sidelines, depressed, enviously observing all the other people whirling about on the dance floor. Finally the instructor came over to me and said something very simple, yet quite important: "Move what you can move."

In other words, despite my condition, I still had some choices to make. I could sit there feeling sorry for myself, watching everybody else, or I could move what I could move. I chose the latter alternative, and began moving only my

49

fingers. As I began dancing with my hands, I realized that I could actually move with my arms. And my head and neck were also free from pain, as were my feet. My bad back was not nearly as incapacitating as I was making it. Through this process of willingly opening up to whatever movement I could muster, my back problem cleared up, quite miraculously, and within a day or two, I was whirling about the dance floor with the best of them. I tell you this story in order to short-circuit any excuse you might have come up with to avoid doing this exercise. If you only have sufficient energy and strength to move your right pinkie for twenty-five minutes, then do that.

So with this in mind—or rather, with nothing in mind at all—please put on your music and begin your dancing now. And do whatever you can do. Be conscious and kind to your body: don't push it beyond its limits and cause yourself harm. But also don't let yourself listen to the voice of inertia and be lazy about this. Only you will know the difference. Those of you who are runners may remember the resistance you probably felt when you first started. Had you listened to that voice of resistance, it would have prevented you from persevering to the point where the "runner's high" could have a chance to enter and permeate your consciousness. The same dynamic applies here; there is a potentially rapturous "dancer's high," but it requires a passionate and energetic surrender. And obviously, this may very well not occur from merely this one brief movement session, but perhaps this experience will plant the seeds of such a possibility.

And now, the lights are dimming, the audience is quiet. Position yourself, press "Play" on your cassette or CD player and as you hear the first strains of music . . . begin.

Thank you. The silent applause of your own Being is deafening. Take a moment to simply be with the energy in your body from all that movement, and to be with your breath and mind. When you are ready, please take fifteen to thirty minutes to sit quietly, meditating, observing your breath. These meditative interludes are vital to our process today; they form the silent backdrop against which the music of our Self-expression can be heard. Please begin.

During these quiet times backstage. I will supply you with some key background information that I hope your character will find useful and be able to incorporate into today's script.

I traveled about for many years leading workshops entitled "The Courage of Self-Expression." Using the expressive arts as my principal teaching tools, I would guide people of all ages and from all walks of life through a series of exercises designed to help them tap into the natural spontaneity and creativity that is available to everybody, regardless of talent, training, or artistic leanings.

From our very first breath, each of us is a naturally unique and original expression of the creative life force; it actually takes quite a bit of training and life experience to lose our innate ability to be spontaneous and creative! There has never been a two-year-old who, when handed a crayon for the first time, replied, "Sorry, I can't draw." Likewise, there has never been a child who, upon being taught "Twinkle, Twinkle, Little Star" for the first time, responded by saying, "Sorry Mommy, I can't carry a tune and I don't really have a good sense of rhythm or harmony. I guess I'm just not very musically inclined."

All of us, as children, had a natural ability to be spontaneously creative, with no self-consciousness, embarrassment, or worry about the results of our expressions. It was only in later years that most of us somehow "learned" that we had no talent, or couldn't carry a tune. Someone told us this along the way and we believed them. Unfortunately, often it was a teacher, whose job as an educator should have been to draw out the talent and genius from within us, rather than pushing it all back down, often forever.

In Bucky Fuller's statement, "We are all born geniuses, and some of us grow up less damaged than others," what exactly has been damaged? Not our genius. Not our Divinity or wholeness as Beings. For those aspects are untouchable in this world, undamageable. The damage most of us suffer from is in our ability to *express* our inherent genius.

But the term "Self-expression" has been greatly misused and misunderstood. To those people who perhaps attended a weekend encounter session, Self-expression has often come to mean regurgitating their worst thoughts and feelings at any time, to anyone who will listen! While legitimate Self-expression may certainly include the conscious communication of fearful or hidden thoughts and feelings, the idea has a higher meaning.

52

Very simply, Self-expression is, "the expression of the Self." This is vastly different from the petty outbursts of hostility that are often perpetrated in the name of honesty and "telling the truth." What does it actually mean to "express the Self"? If we turn to definitions from the dictionary, we find that it means, *to manifest or communicate one's essential identity.*

And what is our essential identity? Philosophers and theologians could argue that point forever, but for our purposes, I define "essential identity" as that person we are in those moments when our hearts are most full and flowing with generosity of spirit, appreciation, and loving-kindness toward all beings and situations; that childlike, spiritual dimension of our original nature that is awake to life, love, and laughter; that part of us which is whole and appreciative of the great Divine Mystery of the present moment. In short, we could say that our essential identity is Love itself.

Ordinarily, most of us are not expressing the Self—we

are not consciously loving. Too many of us, too much of the time, are enshrouded in a cloud of suffering and struggle, and the most Self-expression we ever seem to muster is to moan and complain about everything as we desperately search the self-help section for a way out.

The way out requires great courage, defined as *having that quality of spirit which enables one to act in the presence of fear or danger.* Life is extremely dangerous to human beings. The fear of simply living on the planet Earth can be extraordinary. The actual danger to our physical bodies from disease, accident, attack, and death is enormous. The danger to our fragile hearts in relationships is enough to keep many of us alone and isolated. The danger to our spirits and psyches from reading the daily newspaper is potentially devastating.

It requires unusual courage to dare being fully alive in such a world, where everyone is living a careful life, trying not to disturb the status quo, passively hoping for the best, desperately trying to outwit disease and death.

Who dares to be fully alive in the midst of all that? Psychologist Abraham Maslow once asked his students: "Who among you will be great?"

Astonished by their silence, he then asked: "Well, if not you, who?"

Who will be the great celebrators, the singers and dancers and poets, the laughers and lovers? Who will risk being Zorba, leaping onto tabletops, wildly spinning and offering heart and soul to living the life of fullness and love? Who among us will refuse to buy into the conspiracy of this world that asks us to play small? Often, we'd rather support each other's shortcomings and limitations in order to justify our own misery, so that we can at least suffer in good company.

Many of us grew up in a world in which it truly felt dangerous simply to be ourselves, and so our life became a process of shutting down and developing survival techniques, masks, and facades. We voluntarily chose to close off our spontaneity, our natural creativity, and the effortless "manifestation of our essential identity," just to get by in this world. In short, we stopped loving, and began protecting ourselves instead.

Having "the Courage of Self-Expression" means to harness that "quality of spirit" which enables you to love again, and to do so "in the presence of fear or danger," which is to say, the world as we know it. But courage is not something you can find in a book, nor can you find it anywhere outside of your soul's inner determination. Dare you take a stand for love in this life, and allow your own particular creative expression to flow through you, despite the seeming fear and danger of doing so? The instant that you make such a leap of faith, you join the ranks of greatness. And every moment you continue to hold back and hide your own Divinity, power, and love, you reside in the halls of mediocrity. The difference is courage: to have the willingness to fail, to look foolish, to risk embarrassment, and to have others think what they want about you.

Ordinarily, most of us on a self-help or spiritual path are engaged in what appears to be a long process of unraveling and healing, moving toward some time in the future when we hope our True Self will once again be present and available to us. At that time, we imagine, we will be ready and able to express our Wholeness in loving and creative ways. The Path of the Artist, of the Wild Heart Dancing, is not bound to the world of time in the same way.

Why are the arts such a powerful tool for personal healing? Because most of the things we usually do to try and improve ourselves are rooted in a prior assumption that who we are is somehow fundamentally out of whack and needs improving. Therefore, many self-help methods can be a great trap, because the more we do them, the more they reinforce our original notion that we are somebody who needs to be doing this stuff. For example, people on a diet will subtly reinforce their self-image as fat people every time they refuse a piece of cake.

However, when we approach the arts as our allies and healers in our attempts to express ourselves fully, they, in effect, respond to us by saying, "We can provide the healing you seek, but only when you drop your belief that you need healing and instead surrender totally to True Self-expression and do it now!" Artistic Self-expression is most potent when it emerges from a place of prior satisfaction. The Path of the Artist makes extraordinary demands on the aspirant: it demands the instant cessation of all seeking, and the simultaneous leap into full Self-expression.

In a format such as this, you can only hope to get a taste of the possibilities that creative expression may hold for you in your healing process. If just one of the art forms appeals to you and becomes part of your life, you will find it to be an enormous and valuable gift If you find yourself singing in the shower for the first time in a long while, or dancing in the streets, or writing love poems on the back of grocery lists, you should feel satisfied.

But the audience is growing restless . . . the house lights are blinking, signaling the start of Act II.

55

I consider myself a jazz poet, and I am satisfied with that. What intelligentsia says makes little difference . . . because it's not a question of the merit of art, but a question of spontaneity and joy I say. I would like everybody in the world to tell his full life confession and tell it HIS OWN WAY and then we'd have something to read in our old age, instead of the hesitations and cavilings of "men of letters" with blear faces who only alter words the Angel brought them. . . .[1]

Jack Kerouac

WILD HEART DANCING

Act II: *The Writer at Work: Mind-Jazz*

I do not consider myself a writer, in the ordinary sense of the word. I am a man telling the story of his life, a process which appears more and more inexhaustible as I go on.... It is a turning inside out ... with the result that somewhere along the way one discovers that what one has to tell is not nearly so important as the telling itself....[2]

—Henry Miller

*J*ust as dance can free the body, the art of writing can release the mind. This becomes quite clear when you examine the nature of the human mind.

In various Indian meditation disciplines, the mind has been characterized as "a drunken monkey." This means that it has a tendency to swing from branch to branch without rhyme or reason. The chatter that occurs inside our heads is incessant and constant. Our minds have something to say about everything. They are continuously casting judgment, voicing opinions, remembering things, making plans, rehearsing conversations, or just whirling about in random thought processes. And all of this mental activity is automatic, mechanical, and involuntary. This is very easy to prove. If you believe that your thinking process is voluntary and under your conscious control, then try to stop thinking right now. (Listen to yourself: "Of course I can stop thinking, I'm in charge, watch this ... see, nothing but silence in here, what does he mean my head is full of incessant chatter, that's nonsense ... etc., etc., etc.)

Or, take a moment, and try not to think about giraffes.

Okay begin. (Remember, no giraffes. Anything else is okay. Just don't visualize giraffes or think the word.)

Assuming that you are getting the point and are beginning to see the automaticity of your own mind, let's contemplate some of the staggering implications. If I can manipulate the content of your thoughts by merely uttering the word "giraffe," consider all the things that occur around you each moment of every day which are unconsciously and automatically manipulating, impacting, and otherwise directing the content and direction of your own mind!! It's almost too horrible to consider:

Every magazine cover you notice out of the corner of your eye; every fragment of sound from a passing radio; bits of conversation overheard; every taste and physical sensation; every type of weather; every person and plant, animal and car; every event and situation. All the sights and sounds and smells of every single moment continuously influence the content and direction of your thoughts. *59*

While it is clearly impossible to control our environments in such a way as to totally direct the input into our consciousness, it is possible to have a little choice in the matter. For example, if merely one word—giraffe—can automatically trigger your mind with words, thoughts and imagery, just consider what a whole book can do, which is nothing but words. Or a newspaper. Therefore, like those health-conscious people who carefully watch which foods they allow into their bodies, it is wise to choose one's mental food carefully as well. Over time, the negative impact of violent and unwholesome books, films, and television shows cannot be underestimated. There have already been several well-known studies connecting actual violent acts to the plots of television shows which the perpetrator had recently watched.

So that's the bad news about our minds. And all of the expressive arts are helpful in calming "the drunken monkey." Those moments when you are fully "in your body," dancing with total commitment, energy, and abandon, you'll also realize, when you look back on the experience, that your mind was fairly quiet, if not silent. And the same is true with singing: when you are fully engaged in expressing your heart through song, there is no conscious energy left over to be occupied with thinking. But writing is the specific art form tailor-made for healing the mind, since writing uses the very stuff of the mind—words and thoughts—as raw material for creating art. It is not unlike the rose that grows out of a manure pile.

Now, the good news about our minds is that in spite of their negative similarities, they are also unique. Nobody else in the entire world—past, present, or future—has precisely the same collection of thoughts, ideas, memories, and associations as you have. We have each imprinted a fascinating set of life impressions based on our own personal history and experience, which simply cannot be duplicated. Even twins growing up in the same household have vastly different minds and points of view.

The goal of writing as an expressive practice is to honor this uniqueness.

Most people who think they can't write well, or say that they have "writer's block," are simply unaware of the validity of their own, particular "mind-voice." They struggle along, thinking that in order to be a creative writer they need to somehow become more clever, brilliant, and insightful, never suspecting that they simply need to write down the content of their own minds as it is already occurring, and that that would be truly original work! When all struggle to be unique and different is dropped, one can trust the natural, effortless flow of creativity that is the very essence of originality.

Once again, we look to children as our guides, for they are certainly the least likely among us to "alter words the

Angel brought them." In fact, one might even suggest that children are the very angels themselves, and their first word messages are the essence of poetry. Consider a parent's ecstatic reaction to a baby's first words. Isn't it because this pure being of love has at last chosen to communicate? And to communicate from a natural, uncensored state of inherent wholeness? This is precisely the nature of ecstatic poetry and visionary writing—the ability to somehow reach back through years of "learning" and find that original voice which speaks from innocent love and undamaged self-worth, a voice that knows its own authority.

I have spent years exploring this process, trusting that somewhere under the mire and mud of my overconvoluted and complex adult mind, littered with opinions and judgments and self-criticisms and censorship, there lies buried a true voice, a free voice that is not carefully planning what to say or how to say it. A voice that is not busy devising communications to foster a particular response from others, but rather is as natural as a bubbling brook, spilling over with things to say like an excited child on Christmas morning. By contrast, most of us habitually speak and write as if there is never anything new to be thought or expressed.

Are there new thoughts to think? Is there such a thing as original thinking? Original even to ourselves, in the sense that we haven't thought it before? Yes. It is the language of the inspired state, the language of ecstatic, poetic confession, the language of the child/artist within. Henry Miller describes the moment when he first found his true voice:

> Immediately I heard my own voice I was enchanted: the fact that it was a separate, distinct, unique voice sustained me. It didn't matter to me if what I wrote should be considered bad. Good and bad dropped out of my vocabulary.... My life itself became a work of art. I had found a voice, I was whole again.[3]

It could be said that true writing, like true singing, is giving a voice to love. To the Artist of Being, the speaking voice is a crucial instrument, and the mastery of speaking the language of love is perhaps the greatest art of all. For most of us habitually speak not the language of love, but that of dissatisfaction. We are dull complainers, when we must become poets. Obviously, our words represent our thought and perception; not so obviously, our way of "languaging" literally creates and reinforces our particular way of perceiving reality. Therefore, to awaken the inner poet is to consciously speak a reality of love into existence. As St. Paul put it, "Where there is no love, put love, and you will find love." And if we merely refrain from "altering the words the Angel brings us," this task is effortless.

In order to start this process, here are some writing exercises to loosen up the natural flow of your own thoughts, so that you can begin to simply transcribe them onto paper without thinking about them. Your aim is to wipe out the internal censor, that critical, judging editor in your head who carefully considers all the alternatives and then willfully chooses certain words and rejects others. NO! Don't "alter the words the Angel brings you!" You need to write with the wild freedom of a jazz saxophone player, spilling out his improvisations in waves of spontaneous, unplanned, cascading notes. You need to improvise with your thoughts in such a way that it is literally impossible to make a mistake, because there is no right or wrong, good or bad.

In order to begin to approach this sort of "mental improvisation," you need to work with a certain amount of speed. Just as the jazz player has no time to plan or think out his solo, the jazz poet must also leave no room for the judging censor to enter in and begin making editorial decisions.

Gertrude Stein alluded to this when she wrote:

62

You will write, if you will write without thinking of the result in terms of a result, but think of the writing in terms of discovery, which is to say that creation must take place between the pen and the paper, not before in a thought or afterwards in a recounting. . . .[4]

So the main principle of the following exercises is to always write down the *very first thing* that comes into your mind, regardless of whether it makes sense, regardless of whether you like it or think it's good, creative or worth saying!

Write whatever comes, no matter what.

There is a title of a book which expresses all this perfectly: *First Thought, Best Thought,* by the late Tibetan teacher Chogyam Trungpa. The idea is to cultivate the innocence of "child-mind"—that refreshing way in which a child simply speaks its truth, as contrasted to the careful, stilted way of the average adult. But you can't get to the beauty of your mind unless you're willing to "be with" the ugliness. In order to develop trust in yourself, you need to allow yourself to write down whatever crazy things your mind comes up with.

Some of it may horrify you; some of it may seem hopelessly banal; some of it may sound trite or imitative, boring or repetitive, uninspired or perhaps even unwholesome. You need to let it all come out without passing inspection. As an old Zen saying goes, you need to "cherish no opinion for or against anything" that comes through your mind in these writing exercises.

Let's begin with a very basic stream-of-consciousness "free-write." In a moment you will pick up your pad and pen and begin to write continuously, never pausing to think, for five full minutes. Your pen should never stop moving, so that there's no time to consider what to say next or to figure out the best way to say it. You just spontaneously transcribe whatever thoughts run through your mind as if

63

you were merely a secretary taking dictation. It doesn't need to be sensible or coherent or even meaningful.

If you feel stuck, then immediately write, "I feel stuck right now," and continue with whatever comes to you, such as "I feel stuck and I don't like doing this exercise and I have nothing very interesting to write about anyway and actually I'm beginning to feel hungry and think it's time to eat my lunch hey why do people have a middle toe they never use?" And so on. Anything goes. The purpose is to loosen the linear rigidity of your thinking and allow your mind to have the complete freedom to speak with no pressure to be logical, creative or brilliant. To quote Henry Miller yet again:

> I obey only my own instincts and intuitions. I know nothing in advance. Often I put things down which I do not understand myself, secure in the knowledge that later they will become clear and meaningful to me. I have faith in the man who is writing. . . . One gets nearer to the heart of truth, which I suppose is the ultimate aim of the writer, in the measure that he ceases to struggle, in the measure that he abandons the will.[5]

64

In some ways this exercise is not all that different from the meditation with which we began, in that there is no particular result for which you are aiming; it will merely reveal to you the ongoing, unique mental process that is constantly broadcasting inside your head, and also serves as a warm-up for the creative writing explorations that follow. If you need a starting phrase to get you going, try "Right now I'm thinking about . . ." Please begin your five-minute stream-of-consciousness writing now:

Thank you . . . and now, for the benefit of your studio audience, you're going to do a similar exercise *without* writing it down. Pretend that your audience is calling out "trigger words" to you; your job is to simply stand there (standing makes a difference in performance energy, even with an imaginary audience) and speak extemporaneously, without pausing to think, for at least two full minutes, creating a stream-of-consciousness prose poem in response to each word. For example, if the trigger word is "red" you will simply begin speaking. . . .

"Red . . . is the color of a bad sunburn I got at Fire Island back in the days when I rented a group house on the beach with a bunch of crazy people I was in Primal Therapy with and when we weren't swimming we were screaming. . . ." etc.

So now please play this game ten times, using the following words:

winter

game

rain

women

pillow

driving

silence

father

smell

secret

Now moving downstage to your writing table, you will begin honing some of these wild verbal outpourings into more specific poetic choices. As you read each of the following words, quickly write down the first word that comes into your mind, without thinking about it, even for a second. Please begin.

friend _____	belly _____
blade _____	run _____
meadow _____	fog _____
freedom _____	dance _____
change _____	throw _____
hurt _____	sour _____
August _____	symphony _____
scab _____	nail _____
walk _____	jailer _____
purple _____	lamp _____
clergy _____	video _____
point _____	speech _____
egg _____	frenetic _____
Tuesday _____	Venice _____
carpet _____	intend _____
scream _____	work _____
seven _____	nobody _____
fault _____	sail _____
perfect _____	window _____
scissors _____	quest _____
ocean _____	garbage _____

sweat _____   pretty _____

miles _____   odor _____

trouble _____   book _____

breast _____   money _____

wine _____   hotel _____

photo _____   decide _____

The following exercise is almost exactly the same, except instead of single words, you're going to use phrases of two or three words. Again, respond with whatever phrase first pops into your mind after you read each entry. Please begin.

67

wet city snow _____

open window _____

long flowing robe _____

never again _____

singing softly _____

don't do that _____

she knows better _____

the long road _____

six maple leaves _____

frolicking loudly _____

no more tears _____

still silver shadows _____

crashing white waves _____

short bursts of breath _____

sorry you came here _____

feeling free _____

sordid memories _____

colorful ribbons flying _____

blessing you now _____

water and wind _____

I demand this _____

noticing no one _____

soaring morning gull _____

heart-wrenching sobs _____

silent glances _____

you and I laughing _____

wandering aimlessly _____

huddling cold and alone _____

wild dancer exploding _____

fires of memory _____

fleeting thoughts _____

The next exploration builds on these last two and will gently move you into the realm of effortless poetry. Take three sheets of 8½ by 11 paper and divide each into four pieces. Discard two so that you are left with ten small cards. At the top of each one, write a favorite word, one which evokes real feeling in you because of its sound, its meaning, and your association with it. For example, to most children, "candy" would be a favorite word. Or perhaps "kite" or "swimming." The words you choose will most likely be nouns or verbs. (Very few people have words like "that" or "of" in their top ten!) My list, as an example, includes "icicle," "fire," and "erotic." When you have finished, turn your "deck" of word cards over and shuffle them thoroughly.

What we are engaged in is the music and art of language, using words as sound and color, melodies of thought to caress our tired rational minds. Just as applying a dab of violet-blue or lemon yellow to a canvas can have its own beauty with no conceptual meaning attached to it, words too can be purely evocative without making sense in the usual way. A single clear note from a flute played in an empty cathedral may not mean something specific, but it can nevertheless evoke deep feeling and a grander, wordless sort of *69*
meaning.

With this in mind, turn your deck over and begin writing a poem, using just the words on your cards, in the order they appear. It is your aesthetic choice as to how many words will be on each line of your ten-word "sound poem."

Here is how mine turned out:

> purple clear sacred
> erotic chocolate
> icicle leaf
> Buddha fire
> waterfall

When you have completed this process, shuffle your deck again and repeat this experiment two more times. You will end up with three distinct poems, using the same ten words.

And now your patient coffeehouse crowd is waiting for the reading to begin. Deliver what you have as *one long poem,* in three stanzas. Read it slowly, with attention to the bare bones beauty of sound, and listen to yourself in the same way you might listen to a symphony: not busy mentally trying to figure it out, but simply letting the sounds enter you and move you. And it *is* like a piece of music in that you will undoubtedly hear recurring themes and variations.

Please offer your reading now.

Great. Now go through each card, and just beneath the word at the top, write a single line of poetry using that word. For example, on my "fire" card I wrote,

> "Into the heart of the fire."

And for "erotic,"

> "Your spine twisted in sleep, erotic dreaming."

70   Simple. Do it now.

Once again, turn the cards over and shuffle. Then turn them right side up and write the sentence that appears at the top of your deck across a separate page. This time, before moving to the next card, add a new and original line of your own beneath the one you just transcribed.

In my example, I had "Into the heart of the fire" as my opening line, and before going to my next card, I added, spontaneously, "I gaze, watching my life." I then moved to my next card and added, "Your spine twisted in sleep, erotic dream," and then created a new one to follow, "I see you next to me still, purring," so that I now had the first four lines of a poem, of which the first and third lines came from my cards:

> Into the heart of the fire
> I gaze, watching my life.

> Your spine twisted in sleep, erotic dream,
> I see you next to me still, purring.

In this manner, proceed through your deck, alternating a line from your cards, in the order they appear, with an original line of your own, until you have generated a twenty-line poem.

Are you beginning to sense the effortless joy and poetry of your own soul, starting from just ten words of your choosing? It's quite remarkable. Shuffle your deck and repeat this process one more time. When you are done, again offer the results out loud, standing, to your attentive audience, breathing care and life into your work through the passionate, unrushed manner in which you read. Please begin.

As you probably have already figured out, these cards are mere tools to get your poetry in motion. Soon you can put the tools away and dive right into direct expression. But first, there is one more exercise to do.

Shuffle your cards and turn them right side up. You should see a single word followed by a single line of poetry. Thinking about it as little as possible—using the same first-thought jazz impulses we worked on earlier in the word association—add a second line beneath the first. Then immediately place that card at the bottom of the pile and look at the next one. Again, quickly read it and add a second line. In this manner, go through your deck until the first card reappears. Add a third line, and go through the whole pile again, adding third lines to each card. Do this one more time, adding a fourth line to each. When you are complete, you should have ten four-line poems. In certain cases poetic license may demand that a particular poem be finished after only three lines, and you may choose to leave off the fourth. Others may need a fifth line, and you may add it.

Read these ten poems aloud, with the same commitment as before.

Our work with the cards is complete, but we will conclude our Writer-at-Work portion of the day with one last exercise. You would certainly be well advised, however, to remain attentive throughout the day to the poetic whisperings of your inner voice—during one of the many quiet breaks today you may feel the urge to pick up your pen.

In this last writing exercise you will be responding over and over again to a "trigger" phrase: "Who I really am is . . ." But you need to grasp the full scope of the exercise before jumping in. On the most literal and obvious level, you might choose to respond with the apparent facts of your situation. For example, I might write: "Who I really am is . . . a 41-year old man, sitting at a computer terminal on a Tuesday afternoon in Batesville, Virginia."

Or, you might simply respond with your present thoughts: "Who I really am is . . . tired of doing these exercises and I don't feel very creative anyway and I'm glad the lunch break is coming soon, I wonder how I'll feel tonight. . . ." and so forth.

Your answers can be as short as one word: "Who I really am is . . . sad."

Or as long as a full page of run-on, spontaneous, stream-of-consciousness thought. There are no limits or rules.

You may find yourself tapping into memories: "Who I really am is . . . running along the sand on the lake in New Hampshire, Dad cooking hamburgers on the grill, we're on vacation for a whole week."

Or it may be feelings: "Who I really am is . . . angry that life is so short and I have so much I want to do and on top of everything else, it takes three hours to watch *Amadeus* on my VCR."

So various aspects of your identity may come into play

as you do the exercise: the simple facts of who you are, your rambling and perhaps nonsensical thoughts, feelings, memories, plans, fantasies, or desires: "Who I really am is . . . traveling in the Far East, barefoot and bearded, white loincloth, chanting to the gods."

Remember: "first thought, best thought." Whatever your mind happens to be thinking is the right thing to put down, no matter what! No need to struggle for something different or more poetic than precisely what you overhear in your own head. And you do not have to limit the "I" to yourself in the here and now. Feel free to expand your identity outward, and as you go along, begin to think of the "I" as the personal voice of literally anyone or anything, at any time. It might be the "I" of a maple leaf or of Alexander the Great. Or of a little shoemaker in Tangiers, or a dust particle floating in the air. In other words, let your mind and your imagination expand beyond all limits so that it encompasses 73 all the possibilities of the universe and is no longer bound by the tiny parameters of only your own direct personal experience.

Such accessibility to all possible experience is the breathtaking domain of the sacred poet, connected at the heart to all life. It can be your entree into the realm of ecstatic expression. But I caution you: the road to ecstatic expression is paved with a seemingly endless supply of fairly ordinary stuff, and the way to rev up your poetic engine is through consciously choosing to accept and respect every utterance that emerges along the way, so that your inner voices become less hesitant to begin speaking up and stepping forth.

Some examples of this expanded sort:

"Who I really am is a little brown-skinned girl in burlap running along the riverbank of the Ganges, long, black hair, barefoot, hearing her father splashing nearby."

"Who I really am is a cobblestone road in England somewhere, horse and buggy clip-clopping along carrying some fancy aristocrat in a top hat to a brick church on the hill, the smell of wildflowers."

Give yourself permission to "wax poetic." You have the entire world at your fingertips, from your own little toe to the distant stars. Let each response be exactly as lengthy or as short as it needs to be to "say its piece."

Please respond to the trigger phrase a minimum of fifteen times. Once you find your writing rhythm, you may not want to stop doing the exercise, because you will be so fascinated and intrigued by the things coming out of your own head! Begin ("Who I really am is . . .").

Once again, please read the results aloud. Just as your dance earlier today was an effort to reveal your most naked, word-less truth to God, this reading is an attempt to put words to that same energy of sharing your innermost soul. Therefore, read these lines with passion and authenticity, for it is "who you really are." Begin.

> . . . try, like some first human being, to say what you see and experience and love and lose . . . describe your sor-rows and desires, passing thoughts and the belief in some sort of beauty—describe all these with loving, quiet, hum-ble sincerity . . . and if out of this turning inward, out of this absorption into your own world *verses* come, then it will not occur to you to ask anyone whether they are good *verses* . . . for you will see in them your fond natural possession, a fragment and a voice of your life. A work of art is good if it has sprung from necessity. In this nature of its origin lies the judgment of it: there is no other.[6]

—Rainer Maria Rilke, *Letters to a Young Poet*

Interlude

Take a half hour for a light lunch or snack, followed by either breath meditation or nonstructured, contemplative quiet time. Try to avoid the temptation to "go unconscious" while eating: chew and swallow your food slowly and mindfully, remaining aware of the sensations of hunger, taste, and the point when your stomach (as opposed to your mind) requires no more food. In other words, pay attention—there are no real "breaks" during a retreat.

If you brought a journal with you, this might also be an appropriate time to jot down any of your contemplative musings or insights. Enjoy the quiet; enjoy your solitude.

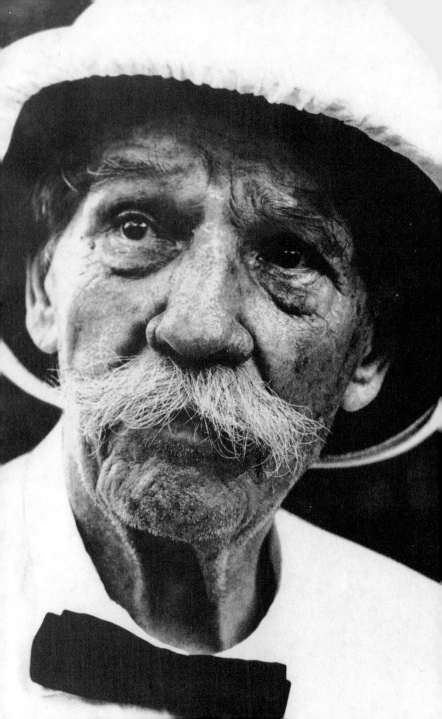

Sometime or another all of us must have found that happy events have not been able to make us happy, nor unhappy events to make us unhappy. There is within each of us a modulation, an inner exaltation, which lifts us above the buffetings with which events assail us. Likewise, it lifts us above dependence upon the gifts of events for our joy. Hence, our dependence upon events is not absolute; it is qualified by our spiritual freedom . . . the triumph of our will-to-live over whatever happens to us.[1]

Albert Schweitzer

WILD HEART DANCING

Self-Inquiry: Fear

Of the world as it is, it is impossible to be enough afraid.

—Adorno

*T*he number one single most powerful archenemy of full Self-expression, the arrow that can painfully pierce the Wild Heart Dancing and render it lifeless, is fear. An instinctive response to living in a world laced with fear is wanting to crawl away and disappear. We think that if we aren't seen, perhaps we will be safe. And yet our soul cries out to be seen, and heard, and danced, and sung, before ourselves and Life. And it isn't safe. But to opt for mere safety is to risk letting our spirit collapse in despair. As Helen Keller said, "Life is either a daring adventure, or nothing."

If you really examined all of your problems and all of the areas in your life that are a painful struggle, you would find that deep beneath the surface the source of your troubles is fear. Nearly all symptoms of distress, worry, and disease in life have fear as the one underlying cause.

While this premise remains questionable among those of a rigidly scientific or medical world view, it is consistently endorsed by a broad spectrum of alternative thinkers, including healers, spiritual teachers, religious leaders, body workers, and other pioneers of this sort.

First, there are the obvious big fears: fear of death, fear of disease and suffering, fear of pain, fear of losing a loved one, fear of financial insecurity, fear of the future. But the list goes on and on: fear of what people think of me, fear of how I look, fear of sex, fear of getting fat, fear of losing my hair, fear of my own dark thoughts and feelings, fear of saying what's on my mind, fear of being exposed or truly seen, fear of being vulnerable, fear of commitment, fear of success, fear of failure, fear of accidents, fear of nuclear annihilation, fear of not fulfilling my destiny, fear of making wrong choices, fear of taking strong action, fear of change, fear of growing old alone, fear of fear, fear of life itself.

And that's just a small sampling of common human fears. I have led many workshop groups through a fear exercise in which we sit in a circle around a single candle, late at night, and quietly share our fears, ritually offering them up to the flame, hopefully to be consumed. If you sat in such a circle, you would find yourself in the company of people from all walks and stations of life—from the nineteen-year-old girl leaving home for the first time, to the forty-five-year-old lawyer in midlife crisis, to the seventy-two-year-old woman who just lost her husband. You would hear a vast spectrum of fear being expressed candidly and honestly, such as:

"I'm afraid to be on my own."
"I'm afraid I'm just drifting and life is passing me by."
"I'm afraid my husband is no longer attracted to me."
"I'm afraid my mother will die before I tell her I love her."
"I'm afraid I'll wind up being a bag lady."
"I'm afraid to meet new people."
"I'm afraid of my sexuality."
"I'm afraid to ask for what I need from people."
"I'm afraid of men's anger."
"I'm afraid of being controlled by women."
"I'm afraid I don't really love my kids enough."
"I'm afraid my body is deteriorating."
"I'm afraid of my tendency toward substance abuse."
"I'm afraid I'm really a bit crazy."

"I'm afraid to be really powerful."
"I'm afraid I'll never get married or have children."
"I'm afraid people will be jealous of me if I really
   succeed."

It goes on and on. The amount of fear that is present in a roomful of people is absolutely staggering. You'd never know it, if you looked only on the surface. If you walked into a cocktail party with that same group of people, you'd probably think everybody was just fine and had their lives pretty much together. Because most of us are so afraid, we spend a good deal of our energy working to cover up our fear!

We learn how to act in this world so that we will be accepted, respected, and liked, but after a while we seem to forget that we are merely acting. So in the process of performing in order to get by and survive, we forget ourselves and lose contact with our own authenticity and essence. We are so busy parading around trying to appear "okay" that we have forgotten what it feels like to truly be okay! We are so busy watching what other people think of us, that we don't really know what we think of ourselves! We are so anxious to appear together and fearless, that we somehow overlook the fact that we are actually living in terror of being found out. For far too many of us humans, far too much of the time, life is a very empty charade in which our carefully constructed "act" meets another's carefully constructed "act," and the two of us simply play out our scene together; no real, genuine, or deep contact or connection is ever made. Our real selves can't get a word in edgewise, because we learned long ago, as children, that it simply wasn't safe to express ourselves, to be true to ourselves, to simply and naturally *be* who we really are.

This is the true tragedy of human existence. Instead of living our lives with passion and expression, daring to be all that we are and truly participate and connect with other beings in a profoundly powerful manner, soul to soul, we have collectively settled for a flat and empty facade, going through the motions of life. The best it ever gets for many of us is when we stimulate ourselves with empty, sensual pleasures in a desperate attempt to feel more alive, or just to feel anything at all! The wild and spontaneous electrical beings that we once were as newborn babies—full of energy and promise—have grown up to become not enlightened and radiant adults but resigned and "endeadened" sleep-walkers.

Often our biggest fear about dying is the unconscious awareness that we have never truly lived; therefore, we fear coming to the end of our lives and facing the realization that we somehow wasted our opportunity here, and it's too late. That is the ultimate human pain: the pain of unfulfilled potential. The pain of not being all that we intuitively sense we could be in this life. The pain of knowing that we came to this world with a purpose and a mission, and the abilities and talents to carry it out, and we somehow lost track along the way and forgot all about it, or else just gave up.

And all because somewhere along the way we became too frightened to really express ourselves and to really put ourselves on the line. We stopped taking chances and ceased to engage in the risky adventure of being fully alive. Instead, we settled for comfort and security, and we paid with our lives.

So that's the bad news: fear. The good news is that human beings need not be the helpless victims of this psychic cancer. There *is* a cure—*love*—and this cure is available to any person who truly wants it.

I learned something very interesting through my experience of rock climbing: fear never exists in the present moment. It only lives in the future. When I am hanging precariously on the side of a mountain, knees shaking and

81

heart pounding, the only way I can calm myself down is to gradually become aware of the fact that in that very instant, I am absolutely safe! I may not know where to put my hands and feet next; I may feel unable to move either further up the mountain or get back down; but in the very moment of now, I am truly safe.

My fear is concerned only with what comes next. And the irony of it is, my fear of the next step compounds my difficulty in finding the next step! It requires a calm perspective to survey one's situation in life and choose the appropriate next move, especially when it is a matter of life or death! So as I settle into the safety of the moment, my heart slows down, my knees relax, I take a deep breath and begin to notice and enjoy the spectacular view and the crisp air . . . and then, miraculously, from that place of trust and appreciation and fearlessness, my next move on the mountain suddenly seems obvious!

82

But I said that the cure for fear is love. What does this have to do with love?

Love is the capacity to choose to be exactly where you are; to embrace and appreciate the present moment of "what is."

Are you hanging from a particular mountain ledge in your life with knees trembling and heart pounding, living in fear? Choose to be where you are. Love the moment you have been given. Relax the desperate search for a solution and breathe a little, look around. The remedy for your fear is not anything that can be found externally. It is not related to altering your circumstances in life. The solution to your troubles and woes is not getting the right job, finding the right mate, earning more money or moving to a better environment. The answer you seek, the healing balm for your wounds, the cure for the demons of fear is already within you, and within each of us. Therefore it is available to you today. It sits right there inside you at this very moment: it is conscious love.

This naturally raises some difficult questions, for certainly there *are* some fear-inducing situations in life for which the only solution *must* be a change of circumstance. Or are there? Here are three very extreme examples that should shed some light on this question:

A friend of mine was traveling through India, feeling lost and unhappy, when a swami he encountered instructed him: "Go seek out one of the many leprous beggars who live on the streets. Find one that appears to be happily alive in spite of his conditions; come back to see me when you've figured out why he's happy."

And so my friend found such a seemingly "miserable" person—a beggar without arms—who in fact projected a radiant, smiling countenance. He spent nearly a month serv- *83* ing as the man's daily companion, sitting on the sidewalk with him, helping to light his cigarettes, feeding him, and so forth. Eventually my friend arrived at the following con- clusion: the "poor" man, either because of his natural dis- position or, more likely, his lack of alternatives, had developed the ability to be "intoxicated with God," able to "choose to love and celebrate the *is* of life," even in the most extreme of circumstances. Presumably he was free to have chosen bitterness as well, but had somehow opted for ecstasy. (Would that we all had his skill in the midst of a traffic jam.) My friend tells me that ever since that experi- ence, he has never again felt truly entitled to indulge in prolonged misery.

Then there was St. John of the Cross, who produced some of his most ecstatic poetic expressions—Divine love poems—while lice-ridden and locked away in a tiny, windowless cell, unheated in winter, unbearably hot in summer.

And finally, there is a book entitled *Hasidic Tales of the Holocaust,* which describes how even in the midst of perhaps the most horrifying and fearful conditions imaginable, there nevertheless were exalted spirits whose faith never flickered for an instant; people who lived and died in the camps without losing their capacity to praise the glory of God in spite of all appearances to the contrary.

Obviously, these are extraordinary human beings in extraordinary circumstances, but they point to the fact that our own fearful situations, which are no doubt a lot less horrific, are potentially manageable through the cultivation of a loving and embracing attitude toward the *is* of our personal predicament, rather than through the reactive and panicky attempt to fix or change it. Hard as it is to root oneself in such an all-encompassing position, it is nevertheless an inescapable fact that the "Awe-ful Mystery of Creation" pervades both the heights and depths of human experience, and when our perception of reality is healed with the "eyes of love," the disease of fear is healed as well.

84

But before we can heal ourselves of a disease, we need to properly diagnose it and examine it very carefully. The next exercise is designed to enable you to become fully aware of all the fears which roam the underground of your consciousness. Please take all the time you need for this exercise, for in many ways it is the most vital step in your process today.

To the best of your ability, truly plumb the depths of your awareness and allow yourself to express any and all fears that come to mind, no matter how silly, remote, irrational, or terrifying. Remember, irrational fears are often the most debilitating kind. For example, there was a woman in one of my workshops who had survived the Holocaust and now lived in a very safe and affluent neighborhood in a suburb of New York City. Despite all her rational understanding, she nevertheless discovered that one of her principal fears in life was that the Nazis were going to break into her house and take her family away. A man who lived in the Midwest discovered that he was afraid that he would be washed away in a tidal wave! One young woman realized she was afraid to experience pleasure.

As you proceed through this exercise, simply relax, explore your thoughts, and let your fears surface. Write down whatever comes to you, even if some of your answers overlap or even repeat themselves. None of this has to make sense or even be logical.

Please pick up your pen and begin now. Use your pad if you need more space.

I'm afraid _____

_____

I'm afraid _____

_____

I'm afraid _____

_____

I'm afraid _____

_____

I'm afraid _____

_____

I'm afraid _____

_____

I'm afraid _____

_____

I'm afraid _____

_____

I'm afraid _____

_____

I'm afraid _____

_____

Relax, take a few deep breaths, and continue.

Another thing I'm really afraid of is _____

_____

Another thing I'm afraid of is _____

_____

I'm also afraid of _____

_____

I never told anyone, but I'm really afraid _____

_____

One of my biggest fears is _____

_____

Is there anything else lurking in there? Anything you're too afraid to write down? Anything you're avoiding? Take a few more minutes and see if you've left anything out.

I'm afraid _____

_____

I'm afraid _____

_____

I'm afraid _____

_____

I'm afraid _____

_____

I'm afraid _____

_____

Thank you. Now imagine that sitting in your audience is a group of very specific, hand-picked people whom you have selected from your entire life: family members, friends, lovers, teachers, enemies, bullies from your childhood, the neighborhood butcher, the "dorm mother" from your college days, and so forth. List their names here first:

87

_____

_____

_____

_____

_____

And now actually visualize each one individually, and exactly where each is situated before you. Is your mom in the front row? Where is your ex-boyfriend or girlfriend? Standing in the back?

Once you have done this consciously and with careful attention, please read this group your list of fears out loud.

• • •

Thank you. That was probably hard work. After an exercise like that, which reveals potentially painful information, the tendency is often to immediately want to "get rid of it," or do something about it. Please just "let it be" for the moment. If your legs are shaking on the mountain ledge of your fears, take a deep breath, slow down, enjoy the view . . . and sing! The process we are engaged in today is not particularly linear; the path of the wild heart follows a logic of the soul rather than of the intellect. And the most logical next step for the soul after contacting one's hidden fears is to sing!

Why?

> Because the cure for fear is love, and . . .
> Love is the expression of essential Self, and . . .
> Singing is a powerful vehicle for Self-expression.

88   Therefore, in the wild heart dancer's approach to life, singing is an extremely logical response to fear!

... and then she begins to sing, and you hear a voice that wells up from the depths of her being, a voice that dwells within her from head to toe, a voice that unfolds like a tall wave of black velvet.[1]

**Jean Cocteau
(speaking of Edith Piaf)**

Alas for those who cannot sing, but die with all their music inside them.

**anonymous,
from a Jewish Prayer book**

WILD HEART DANCING

Act III: *Songs of the Wild Heart*

Life is a cabaret, ol' chum, come to the cabaret.

—from Kander and Ebb's "Cabaret"

*N*otice whether some part of you tightens up with apprehension at the very idea of singing. Although I'm sure there are many of you who are already well aware of the incredible joys of singing, my experience from guiding hundreds of people through workshops is that a great many of us have intense fear and embarrassment about singing, especially in front of others.

Just as dance serves our bodies and provides us with a way to physically unwind and heal, singing is the "friend of the heart," and can be called upon to help purge our repressed emotions and allow our love to flow freely again. Time and again I have witnessed people burst into tears while standing in front of a room attempting to sing. It seems to either trigger painful childhood memories—perhaps when someone told them that they couldn't or shouldn't sing—or else the music itself provokes a deeply emotional response. Music is a powerful healer, if we open to it, and no music is more powerful in this regard than the sound of our own voice in song.

It could be a song of sorrow—the blues—or an angry song of protest and indignation; a gentle love song, or a silly children's song; a Broadway show tune or an American Indian chant. No matter—for every particular feeling state and life situation, there is a perfect song that can help us contact and express ourselves better than any other method I know.

Before we move into the singing portion of this retreat, I must remind you again that you must first surrender all the beliefs you have acquired as an adult, such as, "I can't carry a tune," or, "My voice is terrible," or, "I should only sing in the shower," or, "I'm just not musically inclined," and so forth. Consider the uncritical appreciation we have for a two-year-old's first attempts at singing. Our natural response is delight, for we instinctively perceive that their simple song is a spontaneous expression of beauty and open-hearted love, and it is therefore precious. It doesn't even occur to us to judge it on musical terms, for its true "art-fulness" lies in the love which it expresses.

And is it really any different with "real" art? Consider the expression "sacred music"—the Bach B-minor Mass, for example. My suggestion is that the word "sacred" in this case refers to *a place in consciousness from which the music was created.* Sacred music can only be composed by a composer who, in the act of composing, is in touch with his or her own Being as sacred, and with all life as sacred.

The message for us, as adults who wish to use art as a "Way," or spiritual path, is to use the various practices in order to reconnect to the sacred child within us, whose expressions are inherently original and implicitly sacred in that they emanate from an innocent, long subdued essence of love.

I have found that for me, there is no better way to contact or reconnect with an openhearted interior space than to sing a love song. For there is no activity more unsatisfying, draining, and uninspiring than to sing a love song without love. Merely going through the motions of singing a love song is downright painful. The love song requires and demands love behind it to make it real. And so the practice of singing consistently shows me where I am: either in an inspired, loving state, in which case my singing is a healing

93

experience, or else painfully aware of how cut off I am from my own heart. If I am willing to persist in the practice, the singing of a love song can eventually restore me to the inner space necessary for the song to work.

On the other hand, there is a certain way in which all songs can be love songs, regardless of the actual lyrics or style. Since I've defined true Self-expression as "conscious loving," to the extent that you put your Self totally into a song, it will be, by definition, a love song, a genuine and full expression of who you are. When you really put your heart and soul into a song, without self-consciousness, embarrassment, hesitation, shyness or fear, at that point, to borrow an earlier notion, "the singer disappears, and only the song will remain." That self-conscious voice in your head which is aware that you are singing and is evaluating how you sound is suddenly quiet; in its place, your own authentic, soulful voice sings its truth, directly and without apology. And such naked singing is a powerful gift of love.

To clarify this further, imagine yourself soothing a small, frightened child by singing a lullaby. In such a situation, is there any attention whatsoever on the quality of your voice? "Am I a good singer?" is not even a question that arises, for you are simply grounded in your loving heart, communicating a healing-through-song to the heart of the frightened child. This is how it must be with all real singing, if it is to fulfill its purpose as the "friend of the heart." Whenever we sing, we can tap into that giving place of the lullaby—regardless of the particular style of song—and offer it out to the world.

Perhaps now you can understand the spirit with which you must approach our singing work:

Innocently.
Tenderly.

94

As an offering and gift of the heart.
Not a performance.

Just as it doesn't require a lot of time to step off a high diving board and plunge into space, it likewise doesn't require a lot of time to dive into full Self-expression. It just requires a little courage and a willingness *to step out!* And you can step out at any time, including right now.

Now is as good a time as any, because it's never going to get any easier. If anything, time seems to work against us, in that the more accustomed we are to mediocre lives with stilted Self-expression, the more difficult it can be to dare to change.

DARE TO CHANGE!

This may actually be the most challenging and difficult part of the day for you. It may also be the most important. Because to truly sing out, in full voice and with full breath, without reserve, is to open yourself in a very vulnerable way. At least you have it easy—you're all alone in a room! In my workshops people have to go through this process in front of twenty-five strangers! For most of them, it turns out to be one of the most terrifying experiences of their lives, as well as one of the most healing. (In a research study on human fears, "public speaking" was revealed to be the number one fear for the average person. "Death" came in second!)

Let's begin with some vocal warm-ups, just to get your mouth open, your jaw loose, and audible sounds emerging from within you. Intentionally move and stretch your mouth and jaw as you utter a prolonged "ahhhhh" sound, using one full, deep breath. Do this several times, breathing deeper and longer each time, and allowing the "ahhh" sound to travel up and down your vocal range. Let it soar to a high-pitched falsetto squeak, and let it plummet to a deep, rumbling groan. Next, using your tongue, begin to mumble in gibberish . . . experiment with your voice, and see how many different kinds of sounds you can make, loud and soft, high and low, fast and slow.

Good. Now here's your first assignment: You are a professional actor in a first-run, Hollywood movie. You are playing the part of a nursery-school teacher, and in the scene we are about to shoot, you are going to perform "Twinkle, Twinkle, Little Star" for a group of three-year-olds. (On the off chance that you don't know this song, any children's song will do.) Your job is to sing it fully, at least three or four times through, loudly, expressively, and in a childlike, funny-sounding, pretend voice. (Your "little kid" voice.)

To the extent that you find yourself wanting to avoid, resist, or even skip over this exercise, to that extent are you cut off from the child within you—your innocence and vulnerability, and therefore your love and full aliveness. You really need to be willing to look and feel and sound completely foolish, because most of us have spent the better part of our adult lives trying to look good for others, and avoid looking foolish. The tragedy is, when that approach to life is successful, we wind up looking good on the outside while dying a slow death inside.

Please go ahead and sing the song now—a dozen times, if necessary, until you are truly satisfied that you have given 100 percent and sounded like a happy and free three-year-old with no inhibitions or embarrassment about singing. And allow any emotions to surface in the process—tears, giggles, whatever. Hopefully, there is nobody within earshot to make you self-conscious about this. Singing with your volume turned all the way up is the best way to break through the barriers of inhibition and embarrassment. If there are people who can hear you, and you find that prospect unbearable, it is actually possible to do these singing exercises in an almost whispered voice: what matters more than volume is your intention and commitment of energy. Please begin now.

Thank you. Feel foolish? I hope so. But I'm afraid you're not finished. In fact, it's going to get worse. In the next set of exercises, you will experiment with accessing various emotional qualities in the same song; or, if you prefer, use any nursery rhyme:

(1) **Sing it angrily!** It is quite possible to sing "Twinkle" or "Row, Row, Row Your Boat" with enormous rage. (I once attended an acting class in which a young woman was asked to sing "Over the Rainbow" as if she were an SS officer in the Gestapo!) Anger is easiest to conjure up if you do it loudly, but it can be done at any volume level.

(2) **Sing it as a tender love song.** It is a starry night. You are outside, by a beautiful riverbank, under a full moon, with the love of your life, and you sing your song gently and with great feeling.

(3) **Sing it as if you were in an opera.** Fake a full-bodied, trained voice. (Perform the "Twinkle" aria!)

(4) **Sing it like a rock star.** Pretend to hold a microphone, and imagine 300,000 screaming kids in the audience and a full band behind you. Sing your song in a loud, raucous voice. (If you're inspired, create your own lyrics in the moment . . . it's the energy you put out that counts in these exercises.)

(5) **Sing it with a foreign accent** (British, Yiddish, etc.).

97

(6) Sing it like a nightclub singer doing an up-tempo "swing" number. Pretend you're part of a lounge act, entertaining the cocktail crowd at happy hour.

(7) Sing it to yourself, looking into a mirror.

(8) Sing a spontaneous, stream-of-consciousness, country-western song, with any melody. Tell the story, in song, of one of your important relationships, or an important event in your life. Use a Southern drawl.

(9) Make up some of your own methods.

If you followed the original preparatory instructions for setting up this retreat, you will have come prepared to sing a favorite song which you have memorized. If you failed to do this for some reason, hopefully there is a song that you love already stored in your memory. (I also know that there are probably some readers who have been so cut off from the joy of singing over the years that they could barely remember "Twinkle, Twinkle.")

Your task is to work with the song you memorized in the same way we just worked with the nursery rhyme. That is, choose several approaches to the song, try it in different styles and moods, use a variety of emotions until you have truly played with and explored the possibilities of the song. (Try saying the lyrics, reading them as if they were poetry. This will help you to catch nuances of meaning in the lyrics, which may aid you in choosing how to best communicate the song.) Finally, just sing the darn thing! And see if you can perform it with enough energy and commitment that you feel truly satisfied and complete with it.

There is a certain unmistakable sensation of satisfaction that always accompanies true Self-expression. If you decide to end this next exercise prematurely, and you hear thoughts in your head like, "Oh the heck with it, I'll never really get it, I'm not really a singer," and so forth, then you are copping out and selling yourself short. Because remember, this process is not about "becoming a singer" in the traditional sense. It's about becoming fully human, more alive and expressive, and living from your heart. So it doesn't matter how you sound. It doesn't matter whether you are getting the melody right, or what key you are in. It only matters that you are Alive and In Love, and Wholly Present. Please begin.

Unfortunately, it is next to impossible to conduct a very effective singing workshop in a book format, but you should at least come away from this convinced that *singing can be one of the most powerful tools for your spiritual and emotional health and well-being.* If you are not ordinarily someone who sings, START SINGING!! Sing in the shower, sing in your car, sing along with your favorite songs, sing in the woods, at the beach, atop a mountain. And try all sorts of songs: happy and sad songs, love songs, folk and rock, old standards, lullabys, songs in other languages.

99

You'll begin to discover that different songs produce different alterations in your mood—*if you sing them fully, with your whole heart and soul!* As with most things in life, there is very little value or benefit from halfhearted, noncommitted singing. Over time you may discover how to use singing as a "mood tonic." And it's not always the way you might think; when you're sad, for example, the solution isn't necessarily to make yourself sing a happy song, although sometimes that can work. Often just the reverse is true: allowing yourself to be just how you are—sad—and singing a sad song, will allow the sadness to be more deeply felt and experienced, and this will eventually allow you to let it go and move on to a different emotional state.

While it is generally best to sing songs that do fit how you are feeling, the opposite may be true for you at certain times. Think of Broadway stars who have to sing the same cheerful number every night, no matter how they feel! They cannot afford to be moody, at least not on stage. It is actually an excellent spiritual discipline to force yourself to sing an all-out "up" song, with total energy and enthusiasm, when you least feel like it. This teaches you to have dominion over your feelings. It gives you some choice in the matter, whereas most of the time as soon as our mood swings down, we helplessly follow.

And consider this: how can you possibly remain miserable if you are tap-dancing and belting out "I Got Rhythm"? Or "Singin' in the Rain"? Don't spend another moment contemplating your existence, trying to solve all your problems: Just come alive! "Life is a cabaret, ol' chum, come to the cabaret."

Consider beginning a collection of sheet music. Browse through the selections at your local music store and choose a few songs that have special meaning to you. Perhaps there is a song you remember from your first date that brings tears to your eyes every time you hear it! Or maybe there's a song you fondly remember your father humming all the time. (Or even not so fondly, depending on your family history.) Even a song with a negative association can be a useful and therapeutic one to learn and sing. Just bear in mind when you move forth from this day, that *singing can be a lifeline that connects you to your heart and True Self.*

There is a practice within Hasidism—a mystical branch of Judaism—that involves singing certain wordless melodies over and over again. They are called *nigguns,* and just as a Hindu might use the sound "om" to transport his consciousness to a meditative state, so too, the Hasidim use these sacred melodies as an ecstatic form of prayer. And since they use no words, the music itself allows the singer to bypass the intellect and commune with God directly from the heart center. Author Elie Wiesel has spoken of this:

... [Hasidic singing will] drive it [your soul] out of your self in order that it may rejoin its Source and become one with it in the *Heichel Hanegina,* the *sanctuary of melody*—it's there I await you in a secret promise.

May you someday find your soul relaxing in the "sanctuary of melody."

In the beginning came the secret word—but I digress. The word actually was no secret. It was laughter....

Groucho Marx

WILD HEART DANCING

Act IV: *My Life: Soap or Sitcom?*

My one regret in life is that I am not someone else.

—Woody Allen

*W*ho do you think you are? More than likely, your notion of who you are is comprised of a lot of facts and information: your name, your age, your gender, your nationality, religion, occupation, interests, personality, etc. For example, in my case,

"I am Elliot Sobel, I'm forty-one, I'm a male, I'm American, I'm Jewish, I'm a writer, I play piano and guitar, I'm witty and intelligent, I'm fairly outgoing though sometimes shy, I weigh 170 pounds, I'm a performer and teacher, I've got brown hair and green eyes, I'm a kind person though sometimes an angry and moody person, I'm a son and a brother and an uncle" and so forth.

Before we go on, I'd like you to do the same thing. Take a few minutes and, to the best of your ability, describe who you think you are: how you define yourself in the world, and what distinguishes you from other people. Please do that now:

I am _____

_____

And of course I am _____

_____

Lastly, I am _____

_____

So that should pretty much cover who you think you are in very real, concrete, and specific terms. Now I'd like you to take exactly three minutes—not a second more—and write down your autobiography. Quickly tell your entire life story. Begin at the beginning and end at the end. I know this is an unreasonable and impossible request. Don't think about it. Just do it, and then read it back to yourself, aloud:

Your description above probably contains some of the obvious and basic facts of your biography—it essentially tells *the story* of your life, as you see it. But is it a true story? Is who you really are in your most essential nature truly captured and described by the mere details of your life story and the apparent facts about who you are?

I used to conduct a similar exercise in my workshops in which the participants were given ninety seconds in front of the room to tell their whole autobiography! It was always fascinating to see which events each person would choose to include in the limited time frame given. After doing the exercise myself dozens of times, I began to see that I essentially manufactured a new autobiography each time—all of them true, yet none of them "the whole truth." Sometimes I told my story in terms of all the different jobs I had had over the years; sometimes I discussed each of my relationships; sometimes the different places I had lived. In articulating our autobiography there are several levels to consider:

(1) What actually and literally occurred in our lives.
(2) What we selectively remember about what actually occurred.

(3) The relative inaccuracies of our selective memories.

(4) What we choose to tell of these memories.

So while we may think we are telling the story of our lives, we are actually offering a random sampling of partially accurate, selective memories of true events!

I am suggesting that your life story—and mine—is a bit of a fairy tale and does not offer an authentic portrayal of the main character. Actually, most of our life stories are worse than fairy tales—we have turned them into soap operas, usually filled with tragedy, romance and despair. And just as people can get addicted to watching soap operas on television every day to find out what happens next, most of us are equally addicted to the melodramatic unfolding of our own romantic story line, the daily soap opera of our lives in which we have the starring role.

Just for fun, take the next two minutes to tell your life story again out loud . . . only this time, make it all up! And make it a horrible sob story: "I was orphaned at age two in a shipwreck. . . ." etc. Do that now:

Whether we admit it or not, for many of us, the more dramatically tragic and miserable our real life story is, the better we like it. Notice that they've never made a soap opera about an ordinary, happy, and well-adjusted person who lives simply and joyfully, has healthy, loving relationships and meaningful work! Who would watch such a show? No, we all seem to prefer the drama of suffering, struggle, betrayals, loss, pain, grief, bitterness, and torment. Those are the elements that comprise a good story.

Therefore, many of us have made sure our own story is at least as captivating to us as the soaps. We cannot tolerate the thought of living simple, ordinary, happy lives. We're afraid our ratings will go down and we'll be taken off the air. Our friends will abandon us because we won't be offering them their fix of daily, juicy installments. Nobody in this world is all that interested in hearing about how wonderfully things are going. This world much prefers suffering, conflict, and pain. It's high time we offered people an alternative view of things . . . a funny one, for example!

> A sense of humor, properly developed, is far superior to any religion yet devised.
>
> —Tom Robbins, *Jitterbug Perfume*

I once spent ten days at a Buddhist monastery in Nepal on retreat, struggling to sit still for the four daily meditations, and struggling to understand the lectures that were being translated from Tibetan. At the end of the ten days, the abbot of the monastery, a Tibetan lama, came and spoke to our group for the first time. And what I heard from him in those few moments had a more profound impact on me than the entire preceding ten days. What did he say that could possibly have been so meaningful?

107

Nothing. He simply laughed uproariously. It wasn't his few words that I remember at all—it was that contagious, effusive, and otherworldly laughter of his that pierced the room and got the rest of us laughing uncontrollably as well. At what, we didn't know, but it was as if there was some Ultimate Cosmic Joke of Human Existence and this guy was forever hearing the Divine Punch Line.

His laughter was extraordinary: it was not the bittersweet laughter that covers pain, or the cynical laughter of the depressed or hopeless, or the inappropriate laughter at someone else's expense. Just pure and free, uncontrollable mirth, the laughter of the gods, like a waterfall splashing or a thunderbolt crashing. I vowed to myself that if I ever had the opportunity, I would return to this man and ask that I be his apprentice in laughter, until I too knew what was so funny!

> At the center of all the countries of the world there stands a certain country. That country includes all other countries within it. Within that country there is one city, and that city contains within it all the cities of all the countries of the world. Within that city there is a single house that contains within it all the houses of all the cities of all the countries in the world. Within that house there lives one man, and he contains within himself all the people in all the houses of all the cities in all the countries in the world. And that man laughs at the entire world.[1]
>
> —Rebbe Nachman of Bratslav

Laughter is an essential part of the wild heart dancer's repertoire. Hearty laughter, which literally means "the laughter of the heart," is an expression of spiritual delight, human joy, cosmic absurdity and Divine silliness. A proper laugh diet can heal the body and soul. And by this I mean the true laughter of that person who can be simultaneously aware of both the suffering as well as the joy of being human.

And the most important subject for humor, naturally, is oneself. To take one's life—the story, the suffering, the problems, the quest—as seriously as most of us do, is to perpetuate the very disease for which we are seeking a cure! A workshop leader once observed this very trend in me, and prescribed a remedy of daily cartoons and at least six months in Disneyland! Along similar lines, in the film *Hannah and Her Sisters* the main character cures himself of suicidal despair by watching a Marx Brothers movie!

It is important to remember that "enlightenment" means to "lighten up." How can being serious about lightening up possibly be productive? There is nothing more disturbing than to observe the long-suffering faces of serious "seekers of enlightenment."

SO LIGHTEN UP!

Take the next few minutes to jot down at least five or six of the funniest things you can remember happening in your life. When you write each one down, give it a title, such as, "The time I dropped the noodle pudding."

You don't need to describe the story itself in detail, but the instruction for this exercise is *to think* about each incident in detail, until you have sufficiently re-created in your mind the moment as it originally occurred in such a way that *your contemplation of it causes you at least to chuckle,* if not to laugh out loud. Please do it now.

One of the funniest things I can remember happening was _____

_____

_____ *109*

One of the funniest things I can remember happening was _____

_____

_____

One of the funniest things I can remember happening was _____

_____

_____

One of the funniest things I can remember happening was _____

_____

_____

One of the funniest things I can remember happening was _____

_____

_____

One of the funniest things I can remember happening was _____

_____

_____

Thank you. Now look back over the list and choose the two stories that provoked in you the most audible chuckle as you recollected it, and tell these stories out loud, as if you were a stand-up comic. See if you can make yourself laugh. Feel free to add new material as it occurs to you, to *110* embellish or stretch the truth, or even to out-and-out fabricate elements of the story as you go along. Your goal is to evoke genuine laughter in yourself.

Please know that failing at this exercise can be as useful as succeeding, in terms of growth. I once took a workshop in which the leader instructed us to laugh continuously for twenty minutes! I couldn't do it. As most of the room rolled around the floor, roaring in hysterics, I found myself weeping at my inability to laugh! But I received learning and healing from that process in my own way. Because most of us, in fact, still need to shed a great many tears before our Divinely inspired, contagious laughter can be revealed and released. Accept yourself for wherever you happen to be in this exercise.

. . . and now, live on our stage, that rib-tickling, outrageously funny person . . . YOU!

Paint as you like and die happy.

Henry Miller

WILD HEART DANCING

Act V: *Painting: The Colors of the Soul*

*T*he next area of artistic exploration involves using your watercolors. Whether you are an accomplished artist or someone who feels incapable of effective doodling, please take out your paints and paper and do these next exercises.

Your goal is not to make a pretty picture that you or anyone else will necessarily like; nor is your goal to make a picture that looks realistic or makes sense. Rather, your goal is very simply to experience again what it might feel like to be in kindergarten, discovering the joy and beauty of playing with color, as if for the first time.

Can you imagine the magic and wonder a small child might experience upon discovering he or she can "make" red? And what blue looks like next to it? Black scribbled over it? A yellow face in the corner? An upside-down green sailboat in the middle? No technique, no plan, no "composition or design"—just sheer, innocent fun with color. We turn to painting as the "friend of the soul and imagination." What better metaphor for an Artist of Being than to gaze at a blank sheet of paper and be responsible, moment by moment, for every shade, texture, color and image that gradually fills the space? To paint flexes the muscles of creating without inhibition: clowns can swing from chandeliers and bears can wear underwear! Sandwiches can be as big as skyscrapers and hats can be created to fit six heads at once!

"To paint is to love again," as writer/painter Henry Miller said. To paint fully and freely is to allow the child to live, and to provide a safe arena for the expression of all the hidden corners of the imagination—not only the dancing

bears but the nightmares and secrets as well. I once took a painting class in which we were all gently encouraged to express those things which we were most reluctant to express, and before long the walls were covered with graphic depictions of things that would make the characters in Dante's *Inferno* blush! And so painting serves to loosen the soul from its rigid boundaries.

This exercise can be a lot more difficult for most adults than it sounds. It's even more difficult for highly skilled artists who already know how to paint and draw, just as it can be very difficult for a trained ballet dancer to drop all technique and simply move freely. But for the kind of artistic expression we are doing here today, this is precisely what is being called for: having "beginner's mind," dropping all techniques, preconceptions, rules, expectations, and artistic philosophies, tapping the spontaneous impulses of the present moment, unclouded by history and previous training or beliefs. Henri Matisse expressed this quite simply: "All I thought of was making my colors sing without any heed to rules or regulations."

115

Your paintings may simply be child-like explorations of meaningless colors, designs and forms, or you might also be inclined to include specific content: figures or objects which have a real correlation to people and things of this world. Remember, many of us internalized the phrase, "I can't draw," early on as our first artistic mantra, and to this day, we are able to judge the merit of our artwork only in terms of its realism. Somewhere along the way we discovered that we couldn't accurately represent an external object in a perfectly realistic and photographic way, and we concluded we couldn't draw. We realized that Rembrandt was better than we were, and so we just gave up and dropped out of the competition. There are two very important observations to note regarding this phenomenon:

(1) The ability to draw realistically is a learnable skill. If

someone were willing to put in the kind of long hours which, for example, they might devote to learning a musical instrument, this goal could be reached.

(2) Simply because you may currently lack the patience and/or desire to learn to draw realistically, does not mean that you cannot draw *at all.* Leaping to such an oversimplified conclusion is simply erroneous.

I remind you again that at a younger age, say three years old, there wasn't anything you couldn't draw. If asked to draw your Aunt Mildred in a top hat, suspended upside down on a trapeze bar inside a giant bird cage, you could have done it! And you can recover this unlimited ability to draw whatever comes to your mind in this very instant, if you just drop the adult standards by which you insist on evaluating how things *look;* simply draw exactly what you want and feel.

116   Miller said it this way:

> ... no matter how many times I look at a head, a figure, a house, a mountain, I am never able to put down what I see ... I can't get the hang of it, try as I may.... What's wrong with my eyes and noses—and those weird appendages called ears? Everything. My eyes often resemble the eyes one sees in an optician's window. Made of glass, in other words. Usually they have the stare of a madman. As for hands and feet, generally it is impossible to tell whether they are those of a human or an animal. (A smart thing is to leave them out or conceal them in one way or another.)... Yet here is the strange thing... if the mood is right and the urge strong enough, the picture will come out right even though the houses lie on their sides, people walk with lion pads, boats sail in the sky, rivers run uphill, saints look like madmen and women like cows.[1]

So in the spirit of Henry Miller, let your rivers run uphill, your women look like cows! Obviously, this is not a course in perspective, anatomy, portrait painting, or realism. This is rather a day for Wild Hearts Dancing. Let your brush and colors dance freely across the page without fear of failing. Let your pictures surprise you. Let the moment of putting brush to paper be one of intrigue and discovery, with no editorial overview, no sights set on some goal, no adhering to some carefully executed plan or composition.

The important moment is the magical one of creation— not the future moment when you get to put the thing on a wall and look at it! It's possible no one will ever look at it. You yourself may not ever look at it. So drop all concern about how it looks! And dive into the process like a dancer— when a dance is over, there is nothing left. When a painting is complete, all that's left is a piece of paper with stuff on it. But the actual action and process of painting, like a dance, like a song, is gone forever, and you were either delightfully lost in the process or you missed the point! And the point is the pure joy of Self-expression for its own sake, to "paint as you like and die happy." And paradoxically, to the extent that you do approach your painting with this attitude, the chances are very good that you *will* create something that's worth looking at.

This is why our children's art is hung on the refrigerator. Not because it passes some artistic scrutiny, but because it captures a spark of freedom, of joyful abandon and creative discovery. Like a photo, it points to a moment in time that was precious: the child's spontaneous expression of innate originality. It's so simple and obvious, and yet this childlike ability within us has been so trampled on by the opinions and expectations of the adult world that our access to such natural, unencumbered expression is virtually nil.

While still a beginner, Renoir was once approached by one of his art professors in a rather scornful way: "No doubt it's to amuse yourself that you are dabbling in paint?"

To which Renoir answered: "Why, certainly, and if it didn't

amuse me to paint, I beg you to believe that I wouldn't do it."

And years later, as an old man, Renoir capsulized his extraordinary life as an artist in the most delightfully simple way: "I've had fun putting colors on canvas all my life."

So please get out your paints and spend at least an hour or even two hours painting. Perhaps you might choose to make ten paintings very quickly; perhaps you'll want to spend the entire time working on only one or two. Allow them to be ugly and senseless, if they are. Allow them to be beautiful. The key is to let them happen, watching them emerge before you like dream images from your unconscious.

Try not to stop a painting in frustration if you don't like how it's going. Persist through such resistance and stay with it until it begins to feel better to you. Don't try to correct or cover up any "mistakes." Why? Because if you are in the proper frame of mind, you cannot possibly make a mistake. You would never consider any aspect of a dream to be a "mistake." Rather, you'd probably be interested in every part of a dream—or even a nightmare. And the way to cultivate this frame of mind while painting is to consider all of your efforts acceptable and perfect just as they are, rather than trying to manipulate them to look a particular way. Simply allow them to "come through you," receptive to what happens, rather than aggressively trying to make something happen.

> It is to me the most exciting moment," [says D. H. Lawrence] "when you have a blank canvas and a big brush full of wet colour, and you plunge. It is just like diving into a pond—then you start frantically to swim. So far as I'm concerned, it is like swimming in a baffling current and being rather frightened and very thrilled, gasping and striking out for all you're worth. The knowing eye watches sharp as a needle; but the picture comes clean

out of instinct, intuition and sheer physical action. Once the instinct and intuition gets into the brush-tip, the picture *happens,* if it is to be a picture at all.[2]

Please begin painting. When you're done, save the results to hang on your refrigerator! And don't put away your art materials just yet; you will need them again at the end of the next section. (Your paintings can also provide a great opportunity for a spontaneous writing exercise: simply allow one of them to inspire a poem. Or you may want to write a fragment of poetry on the painting itself.)

If I create with my heart, almost all of my original purpose remains. If it is with my head, hardly anything is left. One should not be afraid of being oneself, of expressing only oneself. If you are absolutely sincere, whatever you do or say will please others. . . . I am a child who is getting on . . . my life seems so amazing to me.[3]

—Marc Chagall

Interlude

Please take at least one hour for eating, meditating, stretching, or walking, writing in your journal, doing nothing. Whatever you choose to do, try to remain mindful, aware, and attentive.

The most beautiful and most profound emotion we can experience is the sensation of the mystical. It is the sower of all true art and science. He to whom this emotion is a stranger, who can no longer wonder and stand rapt in awe, is as good as dead. To know that what is impenetrable to us really exists, manifesting itself as the highest wisdom and the most radiant beauty which our dull faculties can comprehend only in their most primitive forms—this knowledge, this feeling is at the center of true religiousness.[1]

Albert Einstein

WILD HEART DANCING

Self-Inquiry: Appreciation and Purpose

*T*here is a well-known passage that seems to show up on people's refrigerators these days, entitled, "I'd Pick More Daisies." It was written by an elderly woman, and speaks of all the things she would do differently if she could start all over:

"I'd go barefoot earlier in the spring and stay that way later in the fall, I'd eat less beans and more ice cream, I'd pick more daisies. . . ." and so forth. It is the appreciation for those simple things available to all of us every day that will someday become the most meaningful moments of our lives when we look back. It won't be the figures in our bankbook, or our list of great achievements. If you live to a ripe old age and reflect back over your years, what will really be important to you? Chances are that what will in fact be important to you is the quality of the love you expressed to the people most dear to you, and the extent to which you feel you lived fully.

Are you so busy making ends meet that you don't have time to walk under the stars with your child and be mystified? Are you too wrapped up in financial worries to enjoy the pleasure of feeling your hair tossed about in the wind, or the smell of the salt-spray air by the seashore? Are you so preoccupied with rushing out of the supermarket and getting home that you fail to notice that the cashier is another mysterious, living human being with a hidden spark of light just waiting to be fanned by someone who can see it?

One of the simplest religions to practice is to "see God in everything and everyone." Through such "en-Goddened" eyes, the gas station attendant becomes a holy man in disguise, the tree outside your door a nature spirit surrounded by invisible *devas,* and your every action becomes imbued with a sense of higher purpose and Divine inspiration, toward the goal of making Earth "as it is in Heaven." To paraphrase a popular expression, "God is in the eye of the beholder." If you've spent years *looking* for God, you need to start *seeing* God instead.

Through such conscious "seeing" we can transform our world into a place where children do not automatically progress from joyful aliveness to the contracted smallness of adulthood but rather naturally expand ever outward, manifesting their essential beingness with ever-increasing enthusiasm, style, and grace. And then die happy.

The question to consider is: Will you die happy?   *125*

And, since death can come at any moment, the question becomes: **Are you happy now?**

The spiritual demand—the warrior's discipline—is to be happy now, and die happy. Are you willing to take on such a demand? Remember, your only other choice is rather mediocre: it is to remain comfortably where you are, making no waves, never rocking the boat, trying to look good for others and put up a reasonable front, go through the motions, get through the day, survive, do your best, put up with things, hope it all turns out someday. It's not a very attractive choice, though 99 percent of humanity makes it daily. It's truly staggering, when you consider the radiant alternative of living the Truly Human life of conscious loving and spiritual freedom.

The Demand: Be Happy Now and Die Happy.

Live your life in such a way that in your later years you will look back, satisfied and content, confidently knowing that you grasped the essence of what is truly important and meaningful in human life and devoted yourself successfully to that great purpose.

You will have picked the daisies, walked barefoot, loved and laughed fully, celebrated the perfection and mystery and majesty of God's creation through your own gratitude, appreciation, and aliveness. That is all that matters in a human life. Nothing more can be said about it. Your challenge is to let this message sink in and impact your existence at its very core. To let yourself be awakened from the daily sleep of "merely living": the daily grind, the routines, the dullness and boredom, the rat race, the complaints, the apathy, hopelessness and passive resignation, the resentments and regrets and bitterness, the wishing and hoping and struggle, the constant lamenting of the past and praying for a better future.

Give it all up into the Great Moment of Now: have the courage and audacity to stand in the very epicenter of Eternity and be "in the image and likeness of God," to look out at creation and "see that it is good." We have been endowed with the God-like power to declare in our world, "Let there be light," and there will be light! Such is the power of our word, our will, and our choice.

Take a few moments now to write your own version of "I'd Pick More Daisies." Write down the simple things you love to do that perhaps you never get around to anymore. Things like sleigh riding, baking cookies, reading a mystery novel, being massaged, picking apples, rolling down a hill, making Valentines from construction paper and doilies. Compile your own list, and when you leave here today, make sure that you fill your life with the items on your list. Please do it now.

I have experimented with various psychedelic drugs over the years, as part of my quest for deeper meaning and realization. On one occasion I found myself actually experiencing my own death. This is actually not an unusual or unheard-of effect of certain hallucinogens. And yet nothing I had ever heard or read about such "ego death" experiences prepared me for the actual event itself. I quite literally believed myself to be actually, physically dead, and, like Tom Sawyer hiding in the church and witnessing his own funeral, I too clearly felt and observed all the consequences of my passing. I suddenly saw all the beautiful things in my life from which I would be forever separated: my family and friends, my favorite music, the sound of rainfall, etc. I experienced the tragic grief of all my loved ones at my parting, and I likewise saw the perfection of the healing process that would become apparent after the mourning period ended.

I remember watching Jimmy Stewart in *It's a Wonderful Life* as a child. If you have never seen it, it usually airs numerous times around Christmas each year. Briefly, it tells the story of a man who reaches a point of great loss and frustration in his life and wishes he had never been born. His guardian angel grants him his wish, and he gets to spend some time walking about in his prior life to observe the consequences of his never being born. Needless to say, he is devastated by what he witnesses, and he longs for another chance. When he returns to life, his enormous gratitude and appreciation for the tiniest things in life, for even the grumpiest people, is tremendously moving and will bring most holiday viewers to tears.

127

In a sense, my own death experience was very similar. In both cases, the point is clear and simple:

APPRECIATE THIS, HERE AND NOW!

As Joni Mitchell sang,

> Don't it always seem to be,
> that you don't know what you got till it's gone....

Conscious appreciation of *what is* is a powerful spiritual practice. Most people are actively engaged in just the opposite: constant complaining about the way things are. Which is your approach? To the extent that you can be a "conscious appreciator," you will find your life slowing down, and you will discover a quiet sense of calm growing within you as you move about your daily world. To the extent that you are a "constant complainer," life will seem to be ever more frustrating and problematic, and the best you can hope for is a false sense of hope that it will all get better someday. You are a victim of the things you complain about, and you believe that if those things would only go away, you'd have a fair shot at some personal joy. But until they do, you're stuck, and all you have for company is your complaints, as you wait hopefully for the day when things will all fall into place.

128   The grim facts of life are: Things will never fall into place. And even if and when they do, the nature of existence is constant change, and "things" are bound to fall right back out of place soon anyway. So it really doesn't pay to place all your eggs in the basket of ever-changing external circumstances.

Perhaps there was a time you can recall from your childhood when your main problem in life was that the days were too short to do all the things you wanted to do; when bedtime seemed to be much too early, and you weren't the least bit tired yet, and there was certainly a whole lot to stay up for! How different it is for the average adult who just barely gets through their day and for whom bedtime is a welcome reprieve from everyday pain and difficulties. How different it is for the average American, who solves the problem of boredom with hours of TV watching and has seemingly lost all touch with true passion for anything, and for whom sleep always seems more attractive and valuable than anything for which one could possibly want to remain awake.

REMAIN AWAKE!!

Literally and figuratively. When you are spiritually awake and alive to the Present Mystery and Splendor, you will quite naturally choose to be physically awake as well. For it will be obvious to you that *there is no boring moment; there are only bored people.* You can no longer afford to wait for the magic; you can rouse yourself from spiritual slumber and awaken to the magic that is already all around you. Magic, too, is in the eye of the beholder.

Here is a simple lesson in awakening to magic: The next time you are bored with life, study and observe an insect until you are absolutely awestruck and mystified! If you find this doesn't work, you should know that it is because your capacity for magical perception has been dimmed over time, and not from any shortage of magic. There is no scarcity of mystery in our universe. There is only a great scarcity of *129* conscious awareness of mystery. I once heard a guru commenting that he simply couldn't understand people who gaze at the night sky, hoping to see a shooting star, as if the stars themselves, just as they are, were not sufficiently mysterious! The world is as magical as we are, or as dull as our tired minds are.

To the person with open eyes and open heart, just *this* is enough! To the spiritually awake person, "with eyes unclouded by longing," not only is "this" enough, it is magical, mysterious, and perfectly awesome. It is said that when Aldous Huxley—famous author and spiritual explorer—was on his deathbed, his vocabulary had essentially reduced itself to one word: "Extraordinary!" After a lifetime of seeking, he had arrived in a place in his consciousness where he perceived everything and everyone as extraordinary.

Contrast the enchantment of Huxley's perception to most of ours, going through the motions of life, bored and disinterested much of the time, trapped in habits and routines, surrounded by a dull and mediocre reality which we persist in perceiving as banal and mundane, never once suspecting that it is our perception which is at fault, and not reality.

A friend of mine was walking with his three-year-old boy when a butterfly flew by. Amazed and wide-eyed, the child asked, "Daddy, what's that?" My friend, to his credit, offered the following reply: "I don't know, son, but we *call* it a butterfly." Most parents, asleep to the wonder and mystery of all life, would have merely declared, "That's a butterfly." But in his simple, unassuming way, my friend was able to communicate a fundamental truth to his child: that nobody really and truly knows what anything actually *is,* but we have made up convenient names for things in the meantime. What is that amazing flying creature with the colorful, fluttering wings, really? And who are you, really? Who am I?

130   The paradox of "searching for one's true Self" is that the real moment of realization is not a "knowing" so much as it is a "not knowing." The enlightened person finally realizes, clearly, that he or she doesn't know and cannot know who or what anything really is in this universe. They see that humanity has simply superimposed a conceptual framework of words, names, labels, and definitions on what is fundamentally unnameable and unknowable, though ultimately experienceable and be-able.

The ecstatic rapture of the great saints and mystics, ironically enough, does not come from understanding life once and for all. Rather, it comes from the great joyful release of all attempts to figure it out! Their joy comes from embracing what could only be termed a "wise ignorance," and the exclamation of such enlightened ones is "I know that I know nothing!" Such a realization is profoundly humbling and allows for great appreciation, gratitude, and reverence for the tiniest aspects of the phenomenon of existence. Nothing and nobody can be taken for granted. Every living being and every life moment is seen as an essential and integral part of the infinite scheme of things.

THOU SHALT NOT BE BORED

What follows is an appreciation exercise. Try to come up with a list of things you appreciate about life, about yourself, about people you know, about things you love. You may already have uncovered some of these things in your "I'd Pick More Daisies" list. But perhaps you have forgotten how much you enjoy the feel of crisp autumn leaves crinkling under your feet in late October. The pleasure of watching an old black-and-white movie on a rainy Saturday afternoon. The sound of the ocean lapping at the shore. The kindness and generosity of one of your friends. Your favorite pair of red socks. Bubble gum. Search your whole life, from childhood onward, and find things you love and appreciate. Search around your present life, the people you know, the *131* places you love, the activities you enjoy. The little things. The sights and sounds and smells and tastes.

I love and appreciate _____

_____

I love and appreciate _____

_____

I remember fondly _____

_____

It's a pleasure to recall _____

_____

I really enjoy _____

_____

I truly appreciate _____

_____

I love _____

_____

One of my favorite things _____

_____

It's wonderful that _____

_____

One of life's special gifts is _____

_____

I'll always treasure _____

_____

Now particularly appreciate and acknowledge *yourself* for
things you have done and for things you are:
"I acknowledge myself for getting through law school."
"I acknowledge myself for being sensitive."
They might seem insignificant:
"I appreciate myself for brushing my teeth every morning."
They might sound boastful:
"I acknowledge myself for being brilliant."
Be willing to boast and blow your own horn. Try not to
leave anything out. Maybe it's a minor event from your child-
hood that nobody ever noticed:
"I acknowledge myself for learning to skate."
Please begin.

I appreciate myself for _____

_____

I acknowledge myself for _____

_____

I appreciate myself for _____

_____

I acknowledge myself for _____

_____

I appreciate myself for _____

_____

I acknowledge myself for _____

_____

I appreciate myself for _____   *133*

_____

I acknowledge myself for _____

_____

Some other things I love and appreciate about myself and my life and life in general are _____

_____

_____

_____

_____

Thank you. I had a spiritual teacher once who used to
say, "What do you see when you look at a puddle? Do you
see the mud underneath, or the reflection of the moon on
the surface?" In the puddle that is your life, have you merely

been gazing at all the mud and failing to notice the reflection of the moon on the surface? Have you been so committed to being dissatisfied and frustrated and looking for a way out that you've missed the beauty and joy of the way in?

After a lifetime of trying to figure out my purpose in life, I finally stumbled onto it only recently: to cheer up the world. And to help make the world a safe place for children to be born and be themselves. A world in which human beings naturally grow from being magical, spontaneous infants to being magical, spontaneous adults rather than bored and predictable automatons. Where the path of our lives allows us to be ever more conscious and open rather than ever more closed up and protected.

You may feel similarly, and we may be somewhat aligned in our purpose, but I'd like you to articulate your purpose in life in your own words. As usual, let your imagination *134* fly in this exercise. Your responses do not have to be realistic or make sense. Please begin.

My purpose in living is _____

_____

My purpose in living is _____

_____

My purpose in living is _____

_____

My purpose in living is _____

_____

My purpose in living is _____

_____

My commitment to life is _____

_____

My commitment to life is _____

_____

My commitment to life is _____

_____

My commitment to life is _____

_____

What I would like to contribute to life is _____

_____

The essential gift I can offer life is _____

_____

The principal vision for my life is _____

_____

Toward the end of my life, I would like to be able

to say _____

_____

Look over your responses and see if you can consolidate all the answers which ring most true with you into one, concise statement:

My purpose in living is _____

_____

It is very helpful to articulate and remember your purpose. It has been my experience that I always feel most happy and fully alive when I am on track with my purpose in life. Let's take a trivial example. Let's say my purpose for going to the market is to buy groceries for dinner. When I'm in the store, however, I become distracted by other desires, and I end up coming home with a bag of cookies, a magazine, and no dinner. I will most likely feel a sense of dissatisfaction about my trip to the market, for I lost sight of my purpose and didn't accomplish what I set out to accomplish.

In the same way, each day we are either on or off track with regard to our true purpose in life as we have defined it for ourselves! You will clearly feel more satisfied with how you are living and choosing to spend your time when you consciously select the various elements of your life to be in alignment and harmony with your central purpose in life.

136

Using your art materials, please take about twenty minutes to create a visual declaration of your purpose for yourself: a poster to hang on your wall that may contain both words and colorful imagery and that will serve as a daily reminder to you each time your eyes fall on it.

God is a concept by which we measure our pain.

John Lennon

WɪLᴅ HᴇART DANᴄɪɴɢ

Act VI: *God and Forgiveness*

*W*hether you are a devoutly religious person or a confirmed atheist, you have a concept of God that has a powerful impact on your life. The influence of the nonbeliever's concept of "no God" on his choices and behavior is as strong as the effects on the religious person's life of his concept of God.

But the point is, both are human constructs, composed of ideas, beliefs, thoughts, opinions, and experience. The purpose of this next exercise is for you to become more aware of the unexamined conceptual structure you live in with regard to God, or no-God. Please list as many notions about God as you can come up with: things you believe or don't believe, things you've heard or read, philosophical positions you endorse. Some examples might be:

> I believe God is an energy field permeating every atom.
> I think God is a human myth.
> I think God is loving and all-knowing.
> I believe God sees everything I do and hears my thoughts.
> God is an old man with a long, white beard.

And so forth. Really search your mind for all its unconscious assumptions about the nature of God, all your beliefs and ideas, childhood memories and images, etc. Please begin.

•   •   •

Regardless of the concept of God or no-God that forms the basis of your particular philosophical disposition, most of us, as children, had some sort of God-notion. If nothing else, for many of us, God was at least the "hearer" of our bedtime prayers. You may be one of the exceptions—perhaps your parents were more sophisticated in their theology and somehow managed not to automatically invest your psyche with an anthropomorphic concept of God. But most of us in this culture were raised with some concept of God floating around that we took in and with which we formed a relationship.

It is with this relationship that I would like to work. No matter what religious conclusions you have arrived at as an adult, the following two exercises refer to your relationship with the God of your childhood. Please request forgiveness from this God for ten or more things you have done or been in your life. They may have been specific actions or qualities of character. For Catholic readers, this may smack of confession; for Jews, it will be instant Yom Kippur. These may or may not be pleasant associations; the exercise is useful in either case.

141

Forgive me, God, for _____

_____

Forgive me, God, for _____

_____

Forgive me, God, for _____

_____

Forgive me, God, for _____

_____

Forgive me, God, for _____

_____

Forgive me, God, for _____

_____

Forgive me, God, for _____

_____

Forgive me, God, for _____

_____

Forgive me, God, for _____

_____

142

Forgive me, God, for _____

_____

And now please list ten or more things for which *you* are willing to forgive *God.* It can be personal or universal:

"I forgive you, God, for not giving me a better singing voice."

"I forgive you, God, for making death so scary."

Begin.

I forgive you, God, for _____

_____

I forgive you, God, for _____

_____

I forgive you, God, for _____

_____

I forgive you, God, for _____

_____

I forgive you, God, for _____

_____

I forgive you, God, for _____

_____

I forgive you, God, for _____

_____

I forgive you, God, for _____

_____

I forgive you, God, for _____

143

_____

I forgive you, God, for _____

_____

Let's stay with the spirit of forgiveness for a bit longer. All sorts of events have occurred in your life that were somewhat less than wonderful. You've made many mistakes. The people in your life have made many mistakes. Some of your mistakes hurt others; some of the mistakes of loved ones hurt you. Many of us carry around the burden of these pains much longer than necessary. Many adults, no matter how they appear, are still unconsciously locked into a position of revenge toward parents and other loved ones for things that happened years ago. Many people are still trying to "win," prove themselves right, or get even in some way. And nearly all of us continuously berate ourselves for things we did long ago. We are unwilling to let anybody off the hook, including ourselves!

But we must. A hardened heart cannot be a wild dancer, a minstrel-lover. A vengeful mind cannot bask in appreciation of the glorious moment. A stubborn soul cannot delight in creation. Our tendency to harbor resentments toward ourselves and others is a major impediment to our well-being. In the next series of exercises, see if you can contact the spirit of forgiveness and begin to clear your slate of old stuff that no longer needs to be in your way.

We will start with your immediate family, usually the source of our most painful hurts. As an adult, you may have developed very good relations with them. Yet look deeply into your mind and memory anyway and see if there aren't certain events that still constitute a sore spot, a stubborn grudge where the child in you took an angry and hurt position about something and has never budged since. And please know also, that the child in you was *right,* in the sense that you were responding quite naturally to a real or imagined hurtful occasion. But at this point in our lives those inner places of stuckness—resentment, vengefulness, even hatred—no longer serve any positive purpose and only contribute to our own lack of emotional and even physical well-being, albeit unconsciously.

Also, these exercises are useful and appropriate regardless of whether the particular family member is still alive, for the unforgiven moments are most certainly still alive inside us. We'll begin with your father.

I forgive my father for ———————————————

I forgive my father for ———————————————

I forgive my father for ———————————————

I forgive my father for ———————————————

I forgive my father for _____

I forgive my father for _____

I forgive my father for _____

I forgive my father for _____

I forgive my father for _____

I forgive my father for _____

Take a few moments to breathe deeply, and then continue with Mom.

I forgive my mother for _____

I forgive my mother for _____

I forgive my mother for _____   *145*

I forgive my mother for _____

I forgive my mother for _____

I forgive my mother for _____

I forgive my mother for _____

I forgive my mother for _____

I forgive my mother for _____

I forgive my mother for _____

Again, breathe, and continue with one or more of your siblings.

I forgive _____ for _____
        (name)

_____

I forgive _____ for _____

_____

I forgive _____ for _____

_____

I forgive _____ for _____

_____

I forgive _____ for _____

_____

I forgive _____ for _____

_____

I forgive _____ for _____

146 _____

I forgive _____ for _____

_____

I forgive _____ for _____

_____

Next, anybody or any*thing* else: spouses, children, friends, lovers, neighbors, your dog, the weather, the stock market, Richard Nixon.

I forgive _____ for _____
         (name)

_____

I forgive _____ for _____

_____

I forgive _____ for _____

_____

I forgive _____ for _____

_____

I forgive _____ for _____

_____

I forgive _____ for _____

_____

I forgive _____ for _____

_____

I forgive _____ for _____

_____ *147*

I forgive _____ for _____

_____

I forgive _____ for _____

_____

I forgive _____ for _____

_____

I forgive _____ for _____

_____

I forgive _____ for _____

_____

I forgive _____ for _____

_____

And finally, yourself.

It may be something you've *done:*

"I forgive myself for cheating on Frank."

It may be something you've *felt:*

"I forgive myself for hating my little sister."

Or something you have *thought:*

"I forgive myself for thinking my daughter is stupid."

Or *desired:*

"I forgive myself for wanting to sleep with my best friend's wife."

Or *been:*

"I forgive myself for being stubborn."

Begin.

I forgive myself for _____

I forgive myself for _____

I forgive myself for _____

I forgive myself for _____

I forgive myself for _____

I forgive myself for _____

I forgive myself for _____

I forgive myself for _____

I forgive myself for _____

I forgive myself for _____

And now, to get back to God ... once again, regardless of your current religious beliefs, for the purpose of the next exercise, please assume there *is* a personal God, the one from your childhood who created you and knows you more intimately than you know yourself. I want you to write yourself a letter from that God which covers the following items:

(1) Affirms who you are.
(2) Reminds you of your particular qualities, gifts, and life purpose.
(3) Offers support and guidance and love.
(4) Acknowledges and appreciates you—your accomplishments, successes, achievements.
(5) Answers some of your burning questions.
(6) Conveys any other message God might have for you.

> Please do this now: "Dear (your name)..."

Seal the letter in an envelope, address it to yourself, and perhaps give it to a trusted friend to mail to you in three to six months. It will be a nice reminder of your discoveries *149* and work today.

This next and last exercise may be either the most moving or most embarrassing of the day for you. Now that you have imagined what God might have to say to you, I want you to respond...in song! This could be construed as a thinly disguised form of prayer, but it is the free spontaneous prayer of the minstrel-lover, not the prescribed words of liturgy. Your instructions are to simply begin singing to God, in whatever tone or style feels effortless, creating a spontaneous melody as you go along, and communicating anything and everything on your mind at this point in your life. Allow this exercise to take as long as it needs to. You may find yourself discussing your whole life, your dreams and hopes, your laments and sorrows, your desire for forgiveness, your pleas for strength; or you may find yourself simply telling God a few good jokes, just chewing the fat in song, as if you were side by side in a British pub.

Again, do this exercise regardless of your concept of God

or no-God. If you are devoutly atheistic, consider that you are singing to your own highest potentiality, your own aliveness and love, your essential Self. "The word God," Alan Watts wrote, "is more of an exclamation than a proper name. It expresses astonishment, reverence and even love for our reality." Another concept of God which I think is very useful came from a Carmelite monk named William McNamara, who defined God as "Personal Passionate Presence." Those three words sum up our whole day together. So now, with personal, passionate presence, since the song of your soul to God.

I celebrate myself,
And what I assume you shall assume,
For every atom belonging to me
as good belongs to you.

**Walt Whitman,
"Song of Myself"**

WɪLᴅ HEᴀʀᴛ DᴀNᴄɪɴɢ

From my journal:

There is a free Being living inside me—a Radiant, Visionary Genius who is suffocating, demanding freedom . . . total, anarchistic, childish freedom: to dance naked down Broadway, to throw buckets of red and orange paint all over my apartment walls, to listen to Bartók's "Concerto for Orchestra" with my stereo turned up full blast. I need fanfare—loud horns and brass trumpetings to announce my arrival, my re-entry: I am a Writer and a Poet; an Artist, a Singer and a Dancer, and *what I assume you shall assume*. I make love and I feel God; I see Beauty and I know Truth; and in my poor, troubled, frail human heart and soul there lives a deeper than deep sorrow, for I have been in captivity.

I have tried to be normal and nice and I have tried so very hard to get it all together:

to get my head together,	my life together,
my relationships,	my sexuality,
my finances,	my future,
my career,	my health,
my diet,	my plans,

my my . . .

And now I give it all up.
And now I fall apart completely.

And now, Thank God, I surrender to the Heart Cave, where my True Self dwells, and where I control nothing and where the great Nothing controls me, completely. It is the place of real Love, spontaneity, originality, the Essence of my Being, the Primal I-Am-That-I-Am, the Ancient

One. It is the prior and final Home of the great, undif-
ferentiated, unlimited Awareness of the Unborn.

I take a deep breath and relax. If I meet the Buddha on
the road, I grab his hand and dance into the Void—take
a free-wheeling spin through Emptiness and wind up
Nowhere, which is none other than Now/Here.

In the ongoing, daily Art of Being, there is no choreographer telling you what your next step ought to be. There
is no Omniscient Author writing your story for you or giving
you your lines. There is only the blank canvas of each morning, and a full palette of possibilities and creative choices to
make in the present moment. If you can progress toward
mastery of this process, you will become a true Artist of
Being, one whose life is a consciously designed outward
manifestation of a unique inner essence and vision.

Each of our lives is a work of art, a play of color and   *155*
sound mixing in Time and Space, and we must create our
lives in the same manner with which a child plays with
fingerpaints: each day we look out into our crazy, complex
world of possible experience and swish it all around with
our Will and Intuition. Each conscious and unconscious
choice we make arises from conscious and unconscious
desires and instincts, and the life-collage we create in this
way is an original masterpiece of Abstract Expressionism.

For remember what fingerpainting was really all about?
Not the result. Never the result. It was always about the smell
of the paint and the feel of the thick, wet, gushy paint all
over our hands, and the way it all mixed together as we
flowed our hands over the paper.

Would that the shaping of our lives be as ecstatic! Would
that we were as unattached to the result and in love with
the process! For what is life, if not continual process? There
is never any single moment when it all stops and stands still
so that we can gaze at our work and call it finished and sign

our name to it. Rather, it's always moving and changing and we need to cultivate an enjoyment of change itself.

The Inspired Self lives in the heart of each of us, patiently waiting for us to muster up enough courage to go for it, to allow it, to release it. And so I am Nijinsky, you are Van Gogh, my mother is Mary, your father is Blake, the mailman is Mozart, and God is a riddle to be answered only by our full Self-expression on this Earth here and now! There exists a mysterious Self inside you and me that is wild and free and that will remain unknown and unseen and unrealized until and unless we choose to express it—and all it takes to express this Self is the courage to be great.

And remember, I don't measure greatness in worldly terms. To me, a great person is one with a joyful, open heart, a compassionate and generous spirit, and a courageous soul. Someone with an appreciation of the magical moment of now and a capacity to see the extraordinary in the ordinary. Someone who is a loving, conscious co-creator in the collective human mural of existence which we are all continually working on, adding our personal touch wherever we are, merely through being who we are. And perhaps most important, someone with an extraordinary sense of humor.

Nothing in life is more painful and sad to me than to watch a radiantly alive and spontaneous child gradually deteriorate into a pained and withdrawn adolescent and eventually wind up an embittered and suffering adult. That is the negative motion of the human endarkenment process, and it seems to be the natural course of events for far too many of us and our children.

But I am asserting that this downward spiral is not inevitable, nor is it irreversible. That original, childlike quality of unbridled enthusiasm, unpredictability, and effortless creativity is our true human birthright, and it is our responsibility as adults to first heal and restore ourselves and then help create our world as an environment in which others can do the same.

Spiritual rejuvenation or renewal is not a mere abstraction; it exists as a real possibility for those that seek and claim it, and are willing to do what it takes: have the courage to step out and be radically alive.

And by now it should be clear that one of the richest ways to work with this process of awakening is through traveling the path of the artist . . . which brings us to the final moments of our theatrical performance today: the curtain call!

Art is a human activity, whose purpose is the transmission of the highest and best feelings to which men have attained.

Leo Tolstoy

WILD HEART DANCING

Curtain Call: The Path of the Artist

The object, which is back of every true work of art, is *the attainment of a state of being,* a state of high functioning, a more than ordinary moment of existence. In such moments activity is inevitable, and whether this activity is with brush, pen, chisel, or tongue, its result is but a by-product of the state, a trace, the footprint of the state. . . .

Contemplative appreciation of a *trace;* a picture, hearing music, observing a graceful gesture, may cause the spirit to flame up. We care for and treasure the traces of states of greater living, fuller functioning, because we want to live also, and they inspire to living. That is the value of "a work of art." The traces are inevitable. The living is the thing.[1]

—Robert Henri

I spend many hours of my life practicing the creative "let-go": cultivating the free-flowing, inherently satisfying, spontaneous expression of Being, either through song, dance, the written word or painting. I do *not* do this in the spirit of an "artist" perfecting his craft, nor even in the spirit of an artist making a "significant statement" to the world. Rather, I consistently approach each art form as a personal means of discovering my own truth and tapping into the inspired state; it is Self-expression as a meaningful and intensely pleasurable end unto itself. Paradoxically, the more authentically Selfish I am in this practice, the more it seems I *do* both improve my craft *and* have something to offer others.

Thus many times have I known and tasted the ecstatic moment of "no-mind," when the cacophonous clamor of conflicting inner voices temporarily ceases to dominate my conscious attention; moments of enjoying the delightful, effortless flow of creative energy on which my soul seems to thrive. Nevertheless, to this day, if I am home alone, joyfully singing at the top of my lungs, and someone should happen to walk in on me, I will automatically contract my expression, or perhaps stop singing altogether, thus robbing both of us of the experience. If I force myself to continue, my energy contracts because I now know someone is listening and perhaps judging my performance . . . whereas a moment prior, my singing had not been a performance at all, but a celebration, an intimate communication of my essence with its Source.

If one could somehow "go public" with these kinds of private expressions, he or she would be approaching what I have previously defined as "sacred art." Because in the moment of True, Authentic, Uncensored, Childlike, Vulnerable Expression of the Heart and Soul, one automatically touches *161* and resonates with the identical hidden place in all others, who are likewise yearning to liberate that inner essence. Therefore, the more deeply rooted you are in your own Being when expressing your Self, in any form, the more likely you will tap that which is universal and healing, for the sound of truth echos in the soul like a familiar, soothing melody.

Therefore, the Guru on the Path of the Artist is Authenticity, one's own Divine Being. One must finally bow to one's Self with reverent appreciation for the pure gift of life that lies mysteriously unearned at the core of one's essence. And from this heartfelt appreciation of the sacred in oneself, all else is instantly sanctified as well, and all one's creations become holy offerings: your songs become love songs; your writings, love letters; your movements, a dance.

The arts, like other "Ways," are merely useful vehicles to practice this skill of all skills, the "Art of Being." I use the word "practice" not in the tiresome way a beginning piano student might use it (with its overtones of obligation and homework) but more in the manner in which meditators speak of their "sitting practice." Zen students enter their meditation from the point of view that they *already are* "the Buddha nature," and therefore there is nothing for which to strive, nothing to attain. And yet paradoxically, they meditate to attain this insight; they strive for the remembrance that there is nothing for which they need to be striving.

In the same way, the arts-as-spiritual practice is both a longing for and a present expression of, wholeness and inspiration. We *already are* unique and original; there is nothing to attain, save the remembrance of this fact through our creative expressions, when we allow them to flow. We travel the path of the artist in order to get ourselves to the point where we are not trying to get anywhere at all; at last, if we create, it is simply because the bubbling brook of essential Self spills over into artistic expression:

162

> Every stroke of my brush
> is the overflow
> of my inmost heart.

—Sengai, Seventeenth-Century Zen Master

"Overflow" implies that one's cup is full. Through the arts, as in meditation, we practice living from that place in our consciousness which is full, and needs no further practice or striving . . . and we all need to practice this!

I was once the arts instructor at an ecumenical retreat that was also staffed by a Buddhist meditator, a Christian monk, a Sufi sheik and a Jewish rabbi-in-training. Participants were asked to choose one of the four religious traditions and attend a daily practice at five each morning. I couldn't find one that felt totally comfortable to me at the time, and then I realized that as the arts person, I needed to create a daily practice.

From that day on, I led groups at five each morning in the following program: a half hour of movement and dance, a half hour of devotional singing, and a half hour of either journal-writing or watercolor painting. Although I was accused of starting a new religion and pulling people away from the other four morning rituals, it was in fact a wonderful way to start the day, and perfectly appropriate for those who chose the path of the artist.

On the other hand, I personally have never been able to stick to a daily discipline for very long and admire those who do. The predicament of the artist is that we can neither force the Muse to appear on cue nor merely sit around waiting for inspiration. We can't force our spontaneous, creative impulses into a rigid timetable, yet most of us do need to structure our lives in such a way so as to at least provide the opportunity for such possibilities.

But our arts practice must never deteriorate into a tedious endeavor we're "supposed to do." It must forever remain a delightful thing we yearn to do. And you must discover your *163* own individual, unique balance of self-discipline and anarchistic freedom. Productivity and play. Carefulness and carefreeness. But if one or more of the art forms drew you in today, I encourage you to take it on as a practice, in your own way, at your own pace.

> I know artists whose medium is life itself, and who express the inexpressible without brush, pencil, chisel or guitar. They neither paint nor dance. Their medium is Being. Whatever their hand touches has increased life . . . they are the artists of being alive.[2]
>
> —Frederick Franck

I applaud you as a fellow traveler on the daring Path of the Wild Heart, a path which leads toward mastery of the greatest of art forms: the Art of Being. The "art" of the Artist of Being is Love, and Love is a spiritual art form that has the same requirement as the other arts:

TOTAL FREEDOM

Freedom from fear.

Freedom of expression.

Freedom to see the world through the eyes of innocence, the eyes of the heart.

Freedom to move from one moment to the next with conscious fascination, joyful expectation, and eager readiness to laugh at any moment.

Or cry.

Freedom to be Fully Alive.

The following story is from *The Wisdom of the Desert,* compiled by the late Thomas Merton, mystic and monk:

"Abbot Lot came to Abbot Joseph and said: 'Father, according as I am able, I keep my little rule, and my little fast, my prayer, meditation and contemplative silence; and according as I am able I strive to cleanse my heart of thoughts: now what more should I do?' The elder rose up in reply and stretched out his hands to heaven, and his fingers became like ten lamps of fire. He said: 'Why not be totally changed into fire?' "[3]

And from *Tales of a Magic Monastery* by Father Theophane, another mad, mystical monk:

"I had just one desire—to give myself completely to God. So I headed for the monastery. An old monk asked me, 'What is it you want?'

"I said, 'I just want to give myself to God.'

"I expected him to be gentle, fatherly, but he shouted at me, 'NOW!' Then he reached for a club and came after me. I turned and ran. He kept coming after me, brandishing his club and shouting, 'NOW, NOW!'

"That was years ago. He still follows me, wherever I go. Always that stick, always that 'NOW!' "[4]

Those two stories contain everything we need to know:

**Our mission is to become Fire—
Passionate, Wild Hearts Dancing—
And the time to do it is Now!**

Please get out your dance music again and do a final session of movement, putting heart and soul and spirit into the personal passionate presence of your own essential Self. Surrender. Dance your story, become a prayer-in-motion. Please do this now.

As Thoreau lay on his deathbed, it is reported that his somewhat stern and Puritanical old aunt asked him, "Have you made your peace with God?" to which he is said to have smiled and replied, "I did not know we had ever quarreled."

165

I would like to end our time together in the same way we began: with a breath meditation. You've taken stock of a lot of "stuff" today. See if you can let it all be, and for twenty minutes just enjoy the silence of your breath, devoting all your conscious attention to the mere observation of your inhalation and your exhalation. In the world of "just this," your breathing in and out is all there is right now. In this very moment, it is possible to relax into the experience of having "no quarrel with God."

Following this meditation, depending on the time of day and your situation, I recommend you spend the remainder of your retreat just being with yourself: quietly reflecting, silently walking, softly humming, doing something you love, doing nothing at all.

I leave you now to your final moments of silence. The final curtain call is complete. The theater is empty. Thank you, and best wishes on your journey.

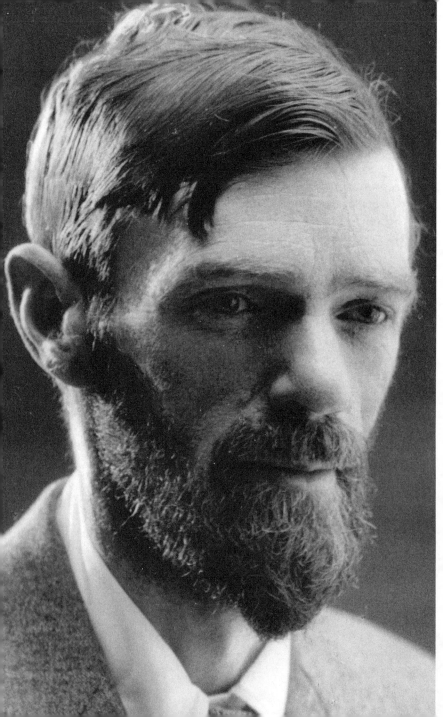

The motto which should be written over every School of Art is: "Blessed are the pure in spirit, for theirs is the kingdom of heaven." . . . This is the beginning of all art . . . be pure in spirit.[5]

D. H. Lawrence

WILD HEART DANCING

Notes

Introduction

1. Holmes, Edward. *Life of Mozart*. New York: E. P. Dutton, 1912.
2. Vonnegut, Kurt. *Bluebeard*. New York: Delacorte Press, 1987.
3. Thoreau, Henry David. *Walden*. Garden City, New York: Anchor/Doubleday, 1973.
4. Emerson, Ralph Waldo. *Self-Reliance*. Mount Vernon, New York: Peter Pauper Press, 1967.

Act I

1. Duncan, Isadora. *Isadora Speaks*. Edited by Franklin Rosemont. San Francisco: City Lights, 1981.
2. Wosien, Maria-Gabriele. *Sacred Dance*. New York: Thames and Hudson, 1974.
3. Ibid.

Act II

1. Kerouac, Jack. *Heaven & Other Poems*. Bolinas, California: Grey Fox Press, 1979.
2. Miller, Henry. *Henry Miller on Writing*. Selected by Thomas H. Moore. New York: New Directions, 1964.
3. Ibid.
4. Preston, John Hyde. "A Conversation." In *The Creative Process*. Edited by Brewster Ghiselin. Berkeley: University of California Press, 1985.
5. Miller, Henry. *Henry Miller on Writing*. Selected by Thomas H. Moore. New York: New Directions, 1964.
6. Rilke, Rainer Maria. *Letters to a Young Poet*. Trans-

lated by M. D. Herter Norton. New York: W. W. Norton, 1962.

Self Inquiry: Fear

1. Schweitzer, Albert. *Reverence for Life*. Edited by Thomas Kiernan. New York: Philosophical Library, 1965.

Act III

1. Lange, Monique. *Piaf.* Translated by Richard S. Woodward. New York: Seaver Books, 1981.

Act IV

1. Green, Arthur. *Seek My Face, Speak My Name*. Northvale, New Jersey: Jason Aronson, 1992.

Act V

1. Miller, Henry. *The Paintings of Henry Miller: Paint as You Like and Die Happy*. Edited by Noel Young. San Francisco: Chronicle Books, 1982.
2. Lawrence, D. H. *Assorted Articles*. New York: Alfred A. Knopf, 1930.
3. Le Targat, François. *Chagall*. Translation by Kenneth Lyons. New York: Rizzoli 1985.

Self-Inquiry: Appreciation and Purpose

1. Einstein, Albert. *The World As I See It*. New York: Philosophical Library, 1949.

Curtain Call

1. Henri, Robert. *The Art Spirit*. Compiled by Margery Ryerson. Philadelphia/New York: J. B. Lippincott, 1923.
2. Franck, Frederick. *The Zen of Seeing*. New York: Random House, 1973.

3. Merton, Thomas. *The Wisdom of the Desert.* New York: New Directions, 1960.
4. Theophane the Monk. *Tales of a Magic Monastery.* New York: Crossroad, 1987.
5. Lawrence, D. H. *Assorted Articles.* New York: Alfred A. Knopf, 1930.

Recommended Reading

Cooper, David. *The Heart of Stillness*. New York: Belltower, 1992.

———. *Silence, Simplicity and Solitude*. New York: Belltower, 1992.

Duncan, Isadora. *Isadora Speaks*. Edited by Franklin Rosemont. San Francisco: City Lights, 1981.

———. *My Life*. New York: Liveright, 1955.

Emerson, Ralph Waldo. *The Portable Emerson ("Self-Reliance")*. Edited by Carl Bode. New York: Viking Penguin, 1981.

Franck, Frederick. *Art as a Way*. New York: Crossroad, 1981.

———. *The Zen of Seeing*. New York: Random House, 1973.

Ghiselin, Brewster. *The Creative Process*. Berkeley: University of California Press, 1985.

Goldberg, Natalie. *Wild Mind*. New York: Bantam, 1990.

———. *Writing Down the Bones*. Boston: Shambhala, 1986.

Hesse, Hermann. *Narcissus and Goldmund*. Translated by Ursule Molinaro. New York: Farrar, Straus & Giroux, 1968.

Kazantzakis, Nikos. *Zorba the Greek*. Translated by Carl Wildman. New York: Simon & Schuster, 1952.

McNamara, William. *Earthy Mysticism*. New York: Crossroad, 1983.

———. *The Human Adventure*. New York: Amity House, 1974.

Miller, Henry. *Henry Miller on Writing*. Selected by Thomas H. Moore. New York: New Directions, 1964.

———. *The Paintings of Henry Miller: Paint as You Like and Die Happy*. Edited by Noel Young. San Francisco: Chronicle Books, 1982.

Nachmanovitch, Stephen. *Free Play*. Los Angeles: Jeremy P. Tarcher, 1990.

Rilke, Rainer Maria. *Letters to a Young Poet.* Translation by M. D. Herter Norton. New York: W. W. Norton, 1962.

Roth, Gabrielle. *Maps to Ecstasy.* With John Loudon. San Rafael, California: New World Library, 1989.

Steindl-Rast, David. *Gratefulness, the Heart of Prayer.* New York: Paulist Press, 1984.

Wilson, Colin. *The Outsider.* Los Angeles: Jeremy P. Tarcher, 1982.

———. *Poetry & Mysticism.* San Francisco: City Lights, 1969.

Wosien, Maria-Gabriele. *Sacred Dance.* New York: Thames and Hudson, 1974.

Recommended Recordings for Movement

Gabrielle Roth & The Mirrors: *Dancing Toward the One, Initiation, Totem,* and others, all composed specifically for "inner dance" and movement-release work. Available from *174* Raven Recording, P.O. Box 2034, Red Bank, NJ 07701. 1-800-76-RAVEN.

About Me (the author)

SJM, 41, *successful* writer and teacher, musician, painter, and performer, funny, creative, prone to angst, never married, never had plants, former editor of *New Sun Magazine,* novel in progress called *MINYAN: The Story of Ten Jewish Men,* fear of intimacy, difficulty with commitment and responsibility, middle-aged hippie with painted car, living in Virginia in country house with artsy friends for $150/month, celibate since Fall '91, didn't read *Iron John,* therapist says I have a *sex-love split,* high cholesterol, rarely floss, led "Courage of Self-Expression" Workshops at Esalen Institute in Big Sur, California and other growth centers, delivered pizza in Hackensack, New Jersey, summer of 1970, busboy in the Adirondacks, summer '71, previous book sold 40,000 copies through mail-order, enjoy receiving massages, not vegetarian (into brisket), never really worked a real job or had a career, performed as comic-actor with The Mirrors in New York for several years, available for screen tests, some people know me as Eliezer, my Hebrew name, . . . SEEKS SF who will mostly leave me alone and bear my children. Prefer someone beautiful, kind, intelligent, spiritual, artistic, sexy, and extremely funny.

(I intend to publish a biannual *Wild Heart* journal celebrating the arts as a spiritual path. For information, please address all correspondence to Elliot Sobel, P.O. Box 2685, Fair Lawn, NJ 07410.)

Photo Credits